1st EDITION

D0603858

Perspectives on Diseases and Disorders

Sports Injuries

Jacqueline Langwith
Book Editor

PERSPECTIVES
On Diseases & Disorders

GALE
CENGAGE Learning

Detroit • New York • San Francisco • New Haven, Conn • Waterville, Maine • London

GALE
CENGAGE Learning

Elizabeth Des Chenes, *Director, Content Strategy*
Cynthia Sanner, *Publisher*
Douglas Dentino, *Manager, New Product*

For more information, contact:
Greenhaven Press
27500 Drake Rd.
Farmington Hills, MI 48331-3535
Or you can visit our Internet site at gale.cengage.com

LIBRARY OF CONGRESS CATALOGING-IN-PUBLICATION DATA

Sports Injuries / Jacqueline Langwith, book editor.
    pages cm. -- (Perspectives on diseases and disorders)
  Summary: "Perspectives on Diseases and Disorders: Each volume in this timely series provides essential information on a disease or disorder (symptoms, causes, treatments, cures, etc.); presents the controversies surrounding causes, alternative treatments, and other issues"-- Provided by publisher.
  Includes bibliographical references and index.
  ISBN 978-0-7377-6358-4 (hardback)
  1. Sports injuries. I. Langwith, Jacqueline.
  RD97.S68834 2014
  617.1'027--dc23

                                      2013035661

Printed in the United States of America
1 2 3 4 5 6 7 18 17 16 15 14

CONTENTS

CHAPTER 3 Personal Experiences with Sports Injuries

FOREWORD

"Medicine, to produce health, has to examine disease."
—Plutarch

Independent research on a health issue is often the first step to complement discussions with a physician. But locating accurate, well-organized, understandable medical information can be a challenge. A simple Internet search on terms such as "cancer" or "diabetes," for example, returns an intimidating number of results. Sifting through the results can be daunting, particularly when some of the information is inconsistent or even contradictory. The Greenhaven Press series Perspectives on Diseases and Disorders offers a solution to the often overwhelming nature of researching diseases and disorders.

From the clinical to the personal, titles in the Perspectives on Diseases and Disorders series provide students and other researchers with authoritative, accessible information in unique anthologies that include basic information about the disease or disorder, controversial aspects of diagnosis and treatment, and first-person accounts of those impacted by the disease. The result is a well-rounded combination of primary and secondary sources that, together, provide the reader with a better understanding of the disease or disorder.

Each volume in Perspectives on Diseases and Disorders explores a particular disease or disorder in detail. Material for each volume is carefully selected from a wide range of sources, including encyclopedias, journals, newspapers, nonfiction books, speeches, government documents, pamphlets, organization newsletters, and position papers. Articles in the first chapter provide an authoritative, up-to-date overview that covers symptoms, causes and effects, treatments, cures, and medical advances. The second chapter presents a substantial number of opposing viewpoints on controversial treatments and other current debates relating to the volume topic. The third chapter offers a variety of personal perspectives on the disease or disorder. Patients, doctors, caregivers, and loved ones represent just some of the voices found in this narrative chapter.

Each Perspectives on Diseases and Disorders volume also includes:

- An **annotated table of contents** that provides a brief summary of each article in the volume.
- An **introduction** specific to the volume topic.
- Full-color **charts and graphs** to illustrate key points, concepts, and theories.
- Full-color **photos** that show aspects of the disease or disorder and enhance textual material.
- **"Fast Facts"** that highlight pertinent additional statistics and surprising points.
- A **glossary** providing users with definitions of important terms.
- A **chronology** of important dates relating to the disease or disorder.
- An annotated list of **organizations to contact** for students and other readers seeking additional information.
- A **bibliography** of additional books and periodicals for further research.
- A detailed **subject index** that allows readers to quickly find the information they need.

Whether a student researching a disorder, a patient recently diagnosed with a disease, or an individual who simply wants to learn more about a particular disease or disorder, a reader who turns to Perspectives on Diseases and Disorders will find a wealth of information in each volume that offers not only basic information, but also vigorous debate from multiple perspectives.

INTRODUCTION

In 1999 the sports network ESPN published a list of the one hundred greatest athletes of the twentieth century. Five of the athletes on the list were from horse racing. Two jockeys were included on the list: Bill Shoemaker, ranked fifty-seventh, and Eddie Arcaro, ranked sixty-sixth. In addition to the two jockeys, ESPN listed three thoroughbred horses; 1973 Triple Crown winner Secretariat was ranked thirty-fifth, ahead of baseball icons Mickey Mantle and Sandy Koufax. Man o' War, who won twenty of twenty-one races in the early 1900s, was ranked eighty-fourth. Citation was ranked ninety-seventh. He won the Triple Crown in 1948 with Arcaro as his jockey. Fans of horse racing are not surprised by the ESPN rankings. They contend that racehorses exhibit courage, strength, determination, and other hallmarks of true athletes. Like other athletes, racehorses also suffer sprained tendons, broken legs, and other sports injuries. Unlike their human counterparts, however, injured racehorses rarely race again. Tragically, most injured racehorses are euthanized or sent to the slaughterhouse. Many people are trying to change this.

On two Saturday afternoons nearly two years apart, millions of people witnessed the heartbreaking injuries of racehorses Barbaro and Eight Belles on national television. In 2006 two weeks after winning the Kentucky Derby, the bay colt Barbaro took a couple of strides at the Preakness Stakes and then collapsed, completely shattering his right hind leg. The crowd at the Pimlico Race Course in Baltimore, Maryland, gasped in horror and then wept. Barbaro endured dozens of surgeries and had pins inserted into his leg, but he was euthanized about eight months later. Eight Belles died at the Kentucky Derby in 2008. Moments after crossing the finish line—right behind winner Big Brown—Eight Belles fell and broke both front ankles. She was euthanized right on the track.

Barbaro and Eight Belles are only two among hundreds of horses that die each year on American racetracks. The organization People for the Ethical Treatment of Animals (PETA) estimates that 700 to 800 injured racehorses die every year. According to the Jockey Club, race-related horse fatalities occurred at a rate of 1.91 per 1,000 starts during the three-year period from January 1, 2009, through December 31, 2011. With over a million starts during this time period, it is estimated that 2,204 horses died.

A March 2012 *New York Times* article revealed the pervasiveness of horse deaths and jockey injuries in horse racing. The *Times* article—titled "Death and Disarray at America's Racetracks"—starts by describing an unfortunately all too common occurrence: a jockey, Jacky Martin, lies sprawled on a New Mexico racetrack, paralyzed from the neck down. Next to him lies Phire Power, his frightened mount, "leg broken and chest heaving . . . minutes away from being euthanized."[1] According to the *Times*, Martin, who made only sixty dollars that day, broke his neck in three places and now lives on a respirator. The very next day, another horse and rider were injured at the same track. The jockey escaped serious injury, but the horse was euthanized. A picture shows the dead horse, Teller All Gone, dumped next to an old toilet in a junkyard.

According to the International Fund for Horses, several factors make injuries to horses particularly devastating. First, strained tendons or hairline fractures are difficult for veterinarians to diagnose. Second, a minor injury can escalate very quickly into a major, or irreversible, injury. Third, horses do not handle surgery well. They tend to be disoriented when coming out of anesthesia and they may fight casts or slings, possibly causing further injury.

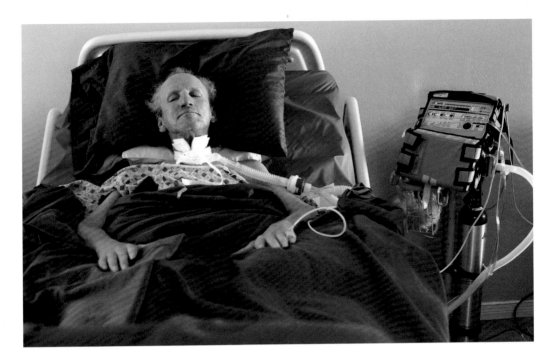

In March 2012 jockey Jacky Martin was paralyzed from the neck down after breaking his neck in a fall during a race. Almost all sports entail the possibility of serious injury. (© AP Images/The El Paso Times, Mark Lambie)

The International Fund for Horses says that instead of going through with surgery, many horse owners choose to save money and simply euthanize the horse. Some callous owners even sell the injured horse for slaughter. Those purchasing injured horses are called "killer buyers." They buy injured horses right at the track and then ship them to slaughterhouses in Mexico and Canada, according to the Humane Society of the United States.

Many people blame doping, the use of performance-enhancing drugs in sports, for the frequency of injuries to racehorses. Doping has gained notoriety for its prevalence in bicycle racing, baseball, and many other sports. It is also rampant in horse racing. Horses are pumped with steroids and a myriad of other drugs—anything, it seems, to increase their speed. Horses are also given addictive medications to mask pain and keep them running even when their muscles are sore. Like human athletes, horses' muscles become fatigued from overuse if they are raced too frequently and do not get adequate rest.

As one of the hundreds of people who commented on "Death and Disarray at America's Racetracks" explained, "As a distance runner, I've noticed my leg injuries are very similar to what horses endure in hard training and it would be crazy to go out and continue speed work with a tendon or bone that's about to "blow." Horses don't have the luxury of saying "stop—I hurt too much to run." And anybody who knows a thoroughbred will tell you these horses will literally run on 3 legs if they can because that's what they're bred to do." According to the International Fund for Horses, doping horses "is not only irrefutably 'cheating,' but also animal abuse."

Longtime horse racing reporter Bill Finley also thinks it is abusive to dope horses. In a September 2012 story for ESPN, Finley contends that horse racing is a broken system "where cheating is rampant, drug testing is inadequate and penalties are usually laughably inadequate. The industry has finally awaken[ed] to these sorry facts, but it needs to take the next logical step, which is to haul these bums away in handcuffs. That's not only what they deserve but a serious deterrent to anyone who thinks it's OK to make their horses run faster through chemical enhancement."[2]

In 2011 and 2012 several US legislators introduced bills to end doping in horse racing and to prohibit the sending of horses to be slaughtered for human consumption. Senator Tom Udall from New Mexico—where a disproportionate number of horse racing fatalities occur, according to the *New York Times*—introduced the Interstate Horseracing Improvement Act, which would have banned race-day medication and racing horses under the influence of performance-enhancing drugs. According to Senator Udall, "Horseracing needs uniform rules to end doping and protect both the integrity of the game and the welfare of horses and jockeys."[3] Legislators from Indiana and Louisiana also introduced the American Horse Slaughter Prevention Act. The act would prohibit the shipping, purchasing, selling, or donating of horses for slaughter for human consumption. None of the legislators' bills were enacted during Congress's 2011–2012 session; however, it is likely the bills will be reintroduced and may be enacted at some later date. According to Finley, ensuring that all horses in the racing industry are well cared for, whether healthy, injured, or retired, will take money and commitment on the part of the horse racing industry. In a column for ESPN titled "Who Will Save the Horses?" Finley says, "Put together enough money and no horse will ever be abused, neglected or slaughtered again. It will take money, but it will more so take a monumental shift in attitude."[4]

While circumstances of injured human athletes may not be as dire and heartbreaking as the circumstances faced by injured horses, it is likely that human athletes will be able to empathize with their four-legged fellow athletes. *Perspectives on Diseases and Disorders: Sports Injuries* provides information on the latest advances in treating sports injuries, commentary about controversial sports injury issues, and personal stories about sports injuries.

Notes

1. Walt Bogdanich, Joe Drape, Dara L. Miles, and Griffin Palmer, "Death and Disarray at America's Racetracks," *New York Times*, March 24, 2012. www.nytimes.com /2012/03/25/us/death-and-disarray-at-americas-race tracks.html?pagewanted=all&_r=0.
2. Bill Finley, "Cheaters: Lock Them Up," ESPN.com, September 25, 2012. http://espn.go.com/horse-racing /story/_/id/8423682/lock-up.
3. Tom Udall, *Fact vs. Fiction: Ending Race Horse Doping*, April 5, 2012. www.tomudall.senate.gov/?p=press_re lease&id=1051.
4. Bill Finley, "Who Will Save the Horses?," ESPN.com, March 22, 2011. http://sports.espn.go.com/sports/horse /columns/story?columnist=finley_bill&id=6247743.

CHAPTER 1

Understanding Sports Injuries

An Overview of Sports Injuries

Maureen Haggerty, Teresa G. Odle, and Rebecca J. Frey

In the following encyclopedia entry Maureen Haggerty, Teresa G. Odle, and Rebecca J. Frey provide an overview of sports injuries. The authors say that children are more prone to sports injuries than adults because their bodies are still developing. The authors discuss the three main types of sports injuries: soft-tissue injuries, skeletal injuries, and brain injuries. On the whole, the authors say, sports injuries are becoming a major public health concern, causing an increase in efforts toward prevention and treatment.

Odle and Haggerty are nationally published medical writers. Frey is a research and administrative associate at the East Rock Institute, an educational research organization.

S ports injuries result from acute trauma or repetitive stress associated with athletic activities. Sports injuries can affect bones or soft tissue (ligaments, muscles, tendons).

SOURCE: Maureen Haggerty, Teresa G. Odle, and Rebecca J. Frey, "Sport Injuries," *Gale Encyclopedia of Medicine,* 4th ed., Ed. Laurie J. Fundukian. Copyright © 2011 Cengage Learning.

Photo on facing page. Between one-half and two-thirds of childhood sports injuries occur during practice or in the course of unorganized athletic activity. (© Greg Wright/Alamy)

Professional dancers are increasingly recognized as performing athletes, and many of the treatments and preventive measures utilized in sports medicine are now applied to dance-related injuries.

It is also important to remember that many types of injuries that affect athletes may also occur in workers in certain occupations; for example, many people in the building trades develop tennis elbow or golfer's elbow. The principles of sports medicine can be applied in the treatment of most common musculoskeletal injuries.

Adults are less likely to suffer sports injuries than children, whose vulnerability is heightened by immature reflexes, an inability to recognize and evaluate risks, and underdeveloped coordination.

In 2002, about 20.3 million Americans suffered a sports injury. Of those, 53% were minor enough to be

This diagram of a hurdler illustrates the variety of injuries that can befall an athlete. (© Carol and Mike Werner/Science Source)

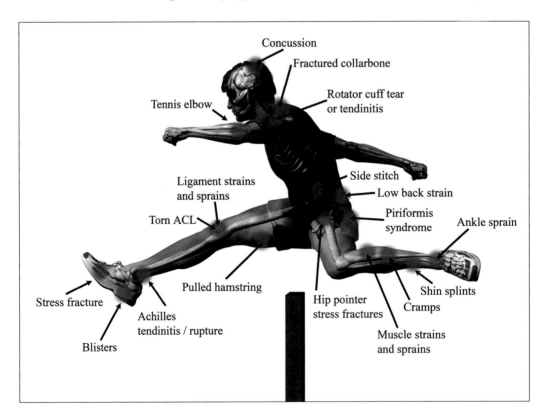

self-treated or left untreated. However, about 10 million Americans annually receive medical attention for their sports-related injuries. That equates to almost 26 per 1,000 people. The highest rate is among children age five to 14 years old (59.3 per 1,000 people). As many as 20% of children who play sports get hurt, and about 25% of their injuries are classified as serious. Boys aged 12 to 17 are the highest risk group. More than 775,000 boys and girls under age 14 are treated in hospital emergency rooms for sports-related injuries.

Injury rates are highest for athletes who participate in contact sports, but the most serious injuries are associated with individual activities. Between one-half and two-thirds of childhood sports injuries occur during practice, or in the course of unorganized athletic activity.

Baseball and softball are the leading causes of sports-related facial trauma in the United States, with 68% of these injuries caused by contact with the ball rather than player-player collision or being hit by a swung bat.

Soft Tissue Injuries

About 95% of sports injuries are minor soft tissue traumas.

The most common sports injury is a bruise (contusion). It is caused when blood collects at the site of an injury and discolors the skin.

Sprains account for one-third of all sports injuries. A sprain is a partial or complete tear of a ligament, a strong band of tissue that connects bones to one another and stabilizes joints.

A strain is a partial or complete tear of:

- muscle (tissue composed of cells that enable the body to move)
- tendon (strong connective tissue that links muscles to bones)

Inflammation of a tendon (tendinitis) and inflammation of one of the fluid-filled sacs that allow tendons to move easily over bones (bursitis) usually result from minor stresses that repeatedly aggravate the same part of the body. These conditions often occur at the same time.

Skeletal Injuries

Fractures account for 5–6% of all sports injuries. The bones of the arms and legs are most apt to be broken. Sports activities rarely involve fractures of the spine or skull. The bones of the legs and feet are most susceptible to stress fractures, which occur when muscle strains or contractions make bones bend. Stress fractures are especially common in ballet dancers, long-distance runners, and in people whose bones are thin.

Shin splints are characterized by soreness and slight swelling of the front, inside, and back of the lower leg, and by sharp pain that develops while exercising and gradually intensifies. Shin splints are caused by overuse or by stress fractures that result from the repeated foot pounding associated with activities such as aerobics, long-distance running, basketball, and volleyball.

A compartment syndrome is a potentially debilitating condition in which the muscles of the lower leg grow too large to be contained within [the] membranes that enclose them. This condition is characterized by numbness and tingling. Untreated compartment syndrome can result in long-term loss of function.

Brain Injuries

Brain injury is the primary cause of fatal sports-related injuries. Concussion, which is also called mild traumatic brain injury or MTBI, can result from even minor blows

> **FAST FACT**
>
> According to the Yale Medical Group, children between the ages of five and fourteen account for 40 percent of sports-related injuries for all age groups.

to the head. A concussion can cause loss of consciousness and may affect:

- balance
- comprehension
- coordination
- hearing
- memory
- vision

Common causes of sports injuries include:

- athletic equipment that malfunctions or is used incorrectly
- falls
- forceful high-speed collisions between players
- wear and tear on areas of the body that are continually subjected to stress

Symptoms include:

- instability or obvious dislocation of a joint
- pain
- swelling
- weakness

Symptoms that persist, intensify, or reduce the athlete's ability to play without pain should be evaluated by an orthopedic surgeon. Prompt diagnosis often can prevent minor injuries from becoming major problems, or causing long-term damage.

An orthopedic surgeon should examine anyone:

- who is prevented from playing by severe pain associated with acute injury
- whose ability to play has declined due to chronic or long-term consequences of an injury
- whose injury has caused visible deformities in an arm or leg.

The physician will perform a physical examination, ask how the injury occurred, and what symptoms the patient has experienced. X rays and other imaging studies of bones and soft tissues may be ordered.

Anyone who has suffered a blow to the head should be examined immediately, and at five-minute intervals until normal comprehension has returned. The initial examination measures the athlete's:

- awareness
- concentration
- short-term memory

Subsequent evaluations of concussion assess:

- dizziness
- headache
- nausea
- visual disturbances

Sports Injury Treatment

Treatment for minor soft tissue injuries generally consists of:
- compressing the injured area with an elastic bandage
- elevation
- ice
- rest

Anti-inflammatories, taken by mouth or injected into the swelling, may be used to treat bursitis. Anti-inflammatory medications and exercises to correct muscle imbalances usually are used to treat tendinitis. If the athlete keeps stressing inflamed tendons, they may rupture, and casting or surgery is sometimes necessary to correct this condition.

Orthopedic surgery may be required to repair serious sprains and strains.

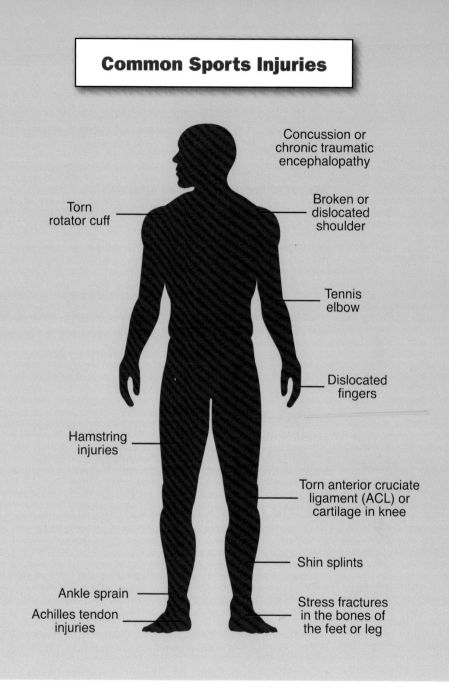

Common Sports Injuries

Concussion or chronic traumatic encephalopathy

Torn rotator cuff

Broken or dislocated shoulder

Tennis elbow

Dislocated fingers

Hamstring injuries

Torn anterior cruciate ligament (ACL) or cartilage in knee

Shin splints

Ankle sprain

Achilles tendon injuries

Stress fractures in the bones of the feet or leg

Controlling inflammation as well as restoring normal use and mobility are the goals of treatment for overuse injuries.

Athletes who have been injured are usually advised to limit their activities until their injuries are healed.

The physician may suggest special exercises or behavior modifications for athletes who have had several injuries. Athletes who have been severely injured may be advised to stop playing altogether.

Sports Injury Prevention

Every child who plans to participate in organized athletic activity should have a pre-season sports physical. This special examination is performed by a pediatrician or family physician who:

- carefully evaluates the site of any previous injury
- may recommend special stretching and strengthening exercises to help growing athletes create and preserve proper muscle and joint interaction
- pays special attention to the cardiovascular and skeletal systems.

Telling the physician which sport the athlete plays will help that physician determine which parts of the body will be subjected to the most stress. The physician then will be able to suggest to the athlete steps to take to minimize the chance of getting hurt.

Other injury-reducing game plans include:

- being in shape
- knowing and obeying the rules that regulate the activity
- not playing when tired, ill, or in pain
- not using steroids, which can improve athletic performance but cause life-threatening problems
- taking good care of athletic equipment and using it properly
- wearing appropriate protective equipment

On a larger scale, sports injuries are becoming a public health concern in America. Prevention efforts include wearing protective devices (such as bicycle helmets and pads when skating or skateboarding), and educating both children and adults about safety. Other preventive efforts include changes in the rules of the game or sport to minimize injuries. For example, wearing goggles will be mandatory in women's lacrosse in order to reverse the rising rate of eye and other facial injuries in that sport. Research also continues on improving equipment. For example, thick rubber insoles can help prevent against repetitive injuries from running but scientists recently observed that they can add to injuries in sports such as soccer, where athletes need to make quick changes of direction. On the other hand, recent improvements in the design and construction of football helmets have been credited with a significant decline in the frequency and severity of head injuries among football players.

ACL Tears Are One of the Most Common Types of Sports Injuries

Jonathan Cluett

In the following article Jonathan Cluett discusses tears of the anterior cruciate ligament (ACL) in the knee. According to Cluett, this injury typically occurs when an athlete pivots or lands after a jump. Torn ACLs are virtually impossible to repair and usually require reconstructive surgery, he asserts. Scientists are trying to understand why ACL tears occur and how best to prevent them.

Cluett is an orthopedic surgeon in Massachusetts. He specializes in sports medicine and arthroscopy and writes orthopedics-related articles for the website About.com.

The anterior cruciate ligament, or ACL, is one of four major knee ligaments. The ACL is critical to knee stability, and people who injure their ACL often complain of symptoms of their knee giving-out from under them. Therefore, many patients who sustain an ACL tear opt to have surgical treatment of this injury....

Most ACL Tears Occur in Sports

An ACL tear is most often a sports-related injury. ACL tears can also occur during rough play, moving vehicle collisions, falls, and work-related injuries. About 80% of sports-related ACL tears are "non-contact" injuries. This means that the injury occurs without the contact of another athlete, such as a tackle in football. Most often ACL tears occur when pivoting or landing from a jump. The knee gives-out from under the athlete when the ACL is torn.

Female athletes are known to have a higher risk of injuring their ACL while participating in competitive sports. Unfortunately, why women are more prone to ACL injury is unclear. . . .

The diagnosis of an ACL tear is made by several methods. . . .

ACL tears cause knee swelling and pain. On examination, your doctor can look for signs of instability of the knee. . . . Special tests place stress on the ACL, and can detect a torn ligament.

An MRI [magnetic resonance imaging] may also be used to determine if the ligament is torn, and also to look for signs of any associated injuries in the knee.

ACL tears do not necessarily require surgery. There are several important factors to consider before undergoing ACL surgery. First, do you regularly perform activities that normally require a functional ACL? Second, do you experience knee instability? If you don't do sports that require an ACL, and you don't have an unstable knee, then you may not need ACL surgery.

There is also a debate about how to treat a partial ACL tear. If the ACL is not completely torn, then ACL reconstruction surgery may not be necessary.

Many patients with an ACL tear start to feel better within a few weeks of the injury. These individuals may feel as though their knee is normal again, but the problems with instability may persist.

This diagram shows an injury to the knee's anterior cruciate ligament (ACL), a common sports injury. (© Nucleus Medical Art, Inc./Alamy)

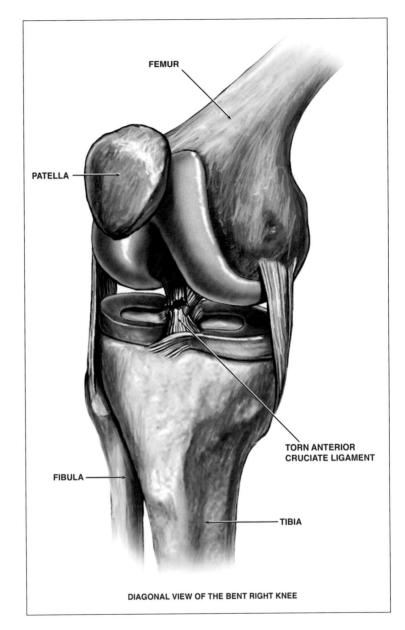

FEMUR

PATELLA

TORN ANTERIOR CRUCIATE LIGAMENT

FIBULA

TIBIA

DIAGONAL VIEW OF THE BENT RIGHT KNEE

The usual surgery for an ACL tear is called an ACL reconstruction. A repair of the ligament is rarely a possibility, and thus the ligament is reconstructed using another tendon or ligament to substitute for the torn ligament.

The are several options for how to perform ACL surgery. The most significant choice is the type of graft used to reconstruct the torn ACL. There are also variations in the procedure, such as the new 'double-bundle' ACL reconstruction [which replaces both parts, or bundles, of the ACL instead of just one].

Risks of ACL surgery include infection, persistent instability and pain, stiffness, and difficulty returning to your previous level of activity. The good news is that better than 90% of patients have no complications with ACL surgery.

Rehab is one of the most important, yet too often neglected, aspects of ACL reconstruction surgery. Rehab following ACL surgery focuses on restoring motion and strength and improving the stability of the joint to prevent future injuries.

While general guidelines exist for ACL rehab, it is critically important that each individual progress through their rehab as their knee allows. Progressing too quickly or too slowly can be detrimental to overall results from surgery, therefore it is important to ensure your therapist and physician are guiding your rehab. . . .

FAST FACT

Young women are two to eight times more likely than young men to injure the ACL, according to the National Institutes of Health website Medline Plus.

ACL Tears Are Particularly Difficult for Athletes

Athletes often have particular difficulty once they have sustained an ACL injury. Many sports require a functioning ACL to perform common maneuvers such as cutting, pivoting, and sudden turns. These high-demand sports include football, soccer, basketball, and others. Patients may be able to function in their normal daily activities without a normal ACL, but these high-demand sports may prove difficult. Therefore, athletes are often faced with the decision to undergo surgery in order to return to their previous level of competition.

ACL tears are often seen in high-profile athletes. Recent athletes who have sustained ACL tears include football player Tom Brady, golfer Tiger Woods, and soccer player Frankie Hejduk.

ACL reconstruction surgery is the standard treatment for young, active people who sustain an ACL tear. But what happens when that person is a child? Should ACL

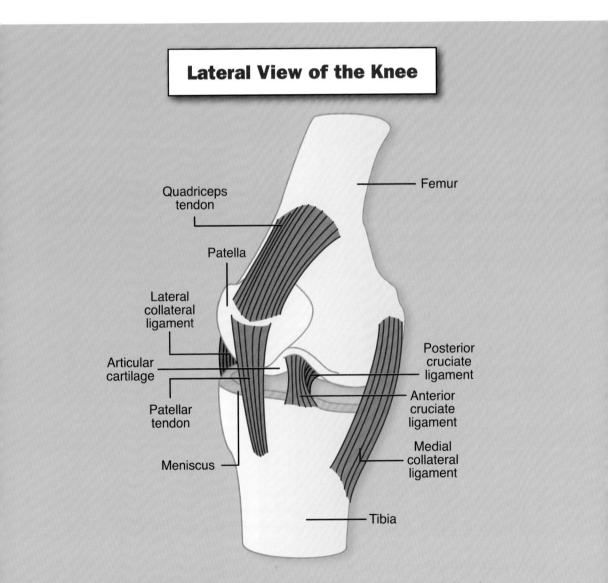

Lateral View of the Knee

Quadriceps tendon

Femur

Patella

Lateral collateral ligament

Articular cartilage

Patellar tendon

Meniscus

Posterior cruciate ligament

Anterior cruciate ligament

Medial collateral ligament

Tibia

Taken from: NIH Publication no. 10–4912., Questions and Answers About Knee Problems. National Institutes of Health, May 2010. www.niams.nih.gov/health_info/knee_problems/default.asp.

surgery be delayed until the child is older, or should ACL reconstruction be performed before skeletal maturity?

The concern of performing ACL surgery in children is that there is a risk of causing a growth disturbance in growing children. Growth plate problems as a result of ACL surgery could potentially lead to early growth plate closure or alignment deformities. However, recent research is showing that the risk of growth plate problems is much less than the risk of permanent knee damage if the ACL is not fixed.

Preventing ACL tears has been the focus of recent research, especially the prevention of ACL tears in female athletes. Numerous theories have been proposed to explain why people may tear their ACL, and how tears can be prevented. Current investigations have focused on neuromuscular training to prevent ACL tears.

Brain Injuries and Collision Sports

Derrick Z. Jackson

In the following article Derrick Z. Jackson discusses chronic traumatic encephalopathy (CTE), a brain disorder that is caused by repeated blows to the head in contact sports. According to Jackson, researchers at Boston University have examined the brains of dozens of deceased athletes—many of whom committed suicide—and have found CTE in most of them. According to Jackson, a brain with CTE when viewed under a microscope looks similar to a brain with Alzheimer's disease. He says the difference between a CTE brain and a healthy brain is stark and should be required viewing for kids thinking about playing contact sports.

Jackson is a columnist and associate editor for the *Boston Globe*, a daily newspaper.

"You see all those brown little things?" [neuropathologist] Ann McKee asked me as I looked through a microscope. I was viewing a slide sample of the brain of Dave Duerson, the Notre Dame All-American defensive back who won Super Bowls with the 1985 Chicago Bears and the 1990 New York Giants. Duerson was a Notre Dame trustee, a National Football League [NFL] Man of the Year for community service, and an economics major who completed a management program at Harvard Business School. Early in his football retirement, he nearly tripled the annual sales of a meat supply company to $63.5 million.

The glory and fortune disappeared in the last decade. An onset of memory loss, hammering headaches, spelling problems, blurred vision, and hot temper led to spousal abuse, divorce, bankruptcy, and, finally, suicide last February [2011] at age 50. In the most eerie recognition yet by an ex-football player as to why he was losing his mind, Duerson shot himself in the chest to preserve his head for research. He left behind the now-famous note, "Please, see that my brain is given to the NFL's brain bank."

Chronic Traumatic Encephalopathy

That brain was sliced open by McKee, a co-director of Boston University's [BU's] Center for the Study of Traumatic Encephalopathy. The "brown things" were nerve cells filled with tau protein, prevalent in degenerating brains like those in Alzheimer's disease. There were so many brown spots, with tails curling off them, that the slide looked like a muddy negative of spinning galaxies.

In that microscopic universe, we were looking into the black hole of contact sports: Chronic Traumatic Encephalopathy [CTE]. This was the hole likely blown into Duerson's head in a career of at least 10 recognized concussions and countless subconcussive hits. This is the void we still let our kids fall into, cheering them all the way.

Due to head injuries sustained while playing pro football, former NFL star Dave Duerson suffered memory loss, hammering headaches, dyslexia, blurred vision, and a heightened irritability that led to spousal abuse, divorce, bankruptcy, and finally suicide. (© **AP Images/ NFL Photos**)

"If it were a normal person, you would see absolutely none of that," McKee said in her lab at the Bedford Veterans Administration Medical Center, where she also runs brain banks for research on military injuries, Alzheimer's, and heart disease. She pointed out how the tails of the tau-infested cells made long projections to make contact with other cells, causing short circuits and disordered thoughts.

"Totally chaos," she said. "I deal with neurodegenerative disease all the time, but you don't see it in 50-year-olds even if you had a gene for the disease."

McKee then showed me a slide of another well-known NFL player who died in his late 70s or early 80s. The constellations of tau were overwhelming. "He's got disease everywhere," McKee said. "There is no place I can go in this brain that's just not incredibly diseased. I've never seen anything like this. This is the worst case I've seen. This guy's brain is 800 grams [in weight], half the size of most players' brains."

A slide from a healthy brain would have had a far more clear background with blue spots. The difference in an injured athlete's brain is so dramatic that the comparisons should be required viewing for parents and youths contemplating high-contact sports and the coaches, athletic directors, and school principals in charge of them. These images should be pinned on the wall with those of blackened lungs we've long used to scare teens from smoking. They just might scare parents and officials into keeping children away from such sports until the sport is changed to minimize head injury.

The urgency grows with each new brain analyzed. In an interview with McKee and her BU Center co-directors, Robert Cantu and Robert Stern, all three say they fear that today's hard-earned concussion awareness, won only in the last couple of years against the prior denial of the NFL, is already being outstripped by new scientific findings.

Chief among them is that the biggest culprit for CTE for many athletes may not be the massive blows that cause concussions but the thousands of lesser ones that do not.

"It gets very scary," McKee said. "In fact, it's gotten to the point where I don't even think about the future. I just report what I see. I think it's going to change things, but I really don't know how it's going to change. I think we have some very concerning information."

It is scary enough that Cantu, who has a book coming out this year [2012] on concussions and children, believes that children under 14 should not play collision sports like football, ice hockey, soccer, and lacrosse until they are modified to eliminate head blows in routine practice and play. "It doesn't make sense to me," Cantu said, speaking for himself and not for the center, "to be subjecting young individuals to traumatic head injury. There's no head injury that's a good one, and you can't play collision sports without accumulating head injuries."

CTE Is Shockingly Common

The BU Center has now analyzed the brains of more than 75 deceased athletes. It has found CTE, originally diagnosed in 1928 in "punch drunk" boxers, in more than 50 of them, including at least 14 of 15 NFL players, and four of six professional hockey players. Evidence of early CTE has now been found in former high school and college football players who died when they were 17, 18, and 21.

The 21-year-old with CTE was Owen Thomas, a popular captain of the University of Pennsylvania football team and a junior in the school's Wharton business program. He committed suicide in 2010 after what friends said was a sudden plunge into depression. He had no history of it, nor of a diagnosed concussion on the football field. But he was a lineman who was known as a hard hitter from the moment he started playing at age 9. He likely took thousands of head blows.

Those circumstances, beyond even the findings in professional athletes, made McKee realize on the day she analyzed Thomas's brain that CTE "wasn't a fluke. This wasn't just a series of horrible coincidences, this was real, this was shockingly common—and it was affecting our kids . . . All I could think of was Owen Thomas, what was going through his mind, was it possible that these changes somehow influenced his decision to take his life?"

NFL Retirees Are More Likely to Suffer from Dementia or Alzheimer's Disease than Other Men

Question: "Have you ever been diagnosed with dementia, Alzheimer's disease, or other memory-related disease?"

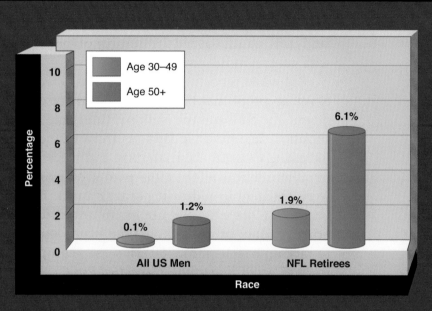

Taken from: David Weir, James Jackson, and Amanda Sonnega. *Study of Retired NFL Players.* University of Michigan Institute for Social Research, September 10, 2009. www.ns.umiich.edu/Releases/2009/Sep09/Final Report.pdf.

Revised Protocols but Continued Violent Play

The evidence to date has forced significant recent changes in contact sports. The NFL, colleges, and state high school athletic associations, including in Massachusetts, have revised or instituted new protocols for taking concussed players off the field and not returning them to play until medically cleared. The NFL recently handed down a precedent-setting one-game suspension for the recent [December 2011] vicious helmet-to-helmet hit by

Pittsburgh Steelers linebacker James Harrison on Cleveland Browns quarterback Colt McCoy.

The NHL [National Hockey League] has also improved its treatment protocol and now penalizes deliberate hits to the head during play. Hockey Canada now penalizes all hits to the head during play, even accidental ones, in the minors (5 to 17 years old) and for females. The Ivy League [a US college conference in New England] this season slashed the number of football practices with contact in full pads.

But while reporting of concussions is way up, there is yet no proof that blows to the head are dramatically down. The NFL and the National Collegiate Athletic Association face multiple lawsuits from former players—including those in their 20s, 30s, and 40s who claim to be suffering from all the hits—who say the organizations were negligent in addressing brain trauma. The NFL last year [2011] gave the BU Center an unrestricted $1 million to further its research, but the league also continued to rack up concussions, 260 last season compared to 200 in 2008, according to the *Associated Press.*

After the Browns became the latest team to botch a concussion diagnosis—with team medical staff saying it missed McCoy being flattened by Harrison—the league decided to put an independent trainer in the press box to survey the action. But that change falls short of the critics' call for an independent neurologist on the sidelines. For a $9 billion enterprise, that would seem to be a small price to pay for medical credibility.

Play remains so violent in the NHL that at one point in mid-December [2011], 23 players were out with concussions. Three weeks ago [December 2011], Rajendra Kale, the interim editor-in-chief of the *Canadian Medical Association Journal,* called for the banning of fighting in hockey, citing BU's research that repetitive head trauma of any kind may contribute to CTE. Three of the four deceased hockey players found to have CTE were "enforcers," known for fighting, including 28-year-old Derek Boogaard.

The *Journal's* editorial came two weeks after NHL commissioner Gary Bettman dismissed connections between concussions and CTE, and downplayed head trauma in fighting, saying, "Our fans tell us they like the level of physicality in our game." But calls to end fighting are growing from within. David Branch, the president of the Canadian Hockey League, which is the prime feeder league for the NHL, which has much tougher penalties against fighting, this month [January 2012] told the *National Post* that, "The time will come where [fighting] will be deemed to be totally unacceptable."

And Hall of Fame goaltender Ken Dryden criticized Bettman's level of denial in a December essay in the *Toronto Globe and Mail*, saying, "That's how thousands of asbestos workers and millions of smokers died."

It Begins in Youth Sports

Nothing the NFL or NHL does can begin to address where brain trauma actually starts in many cases: youth sports. A Centers for Disease Control and Prevention [CDC] report in October [2011] found that virtually the same number of youths ages 10 to 14 (60,272) annually go to emergency rooms for nonfatal traumatic brain injuries [TBIs] as youths 15 to 19 (61,851).

For boys, the top cause in both age groups was football. For girls, the top cause at 10 to 14 was bicycling. By 15 to 19, it was soccer. Other significant causes for girls 10 to 19 were basketball and gymnastics.

Emergency room [ER] visits for youth sports-related traumatic brain injuries overall went up 62 percent from 2001 to 2009. Much of that rise likely represents much better concussion awareness. But researchers also believe it represents athletes continuing to get bigger, faster, and stronger—and sports officials not adjusting their rules fast enough to mitigate the damage. This makes no sense when, according to the CDC, "younger persons are at increased risk for TBIs with increased severity and prolonged recovery."

Those ER visits scream for us to hear the silent story. In ongoing research, a Purdue University engineering team, using accelerometers in football helmets and before-and-after brain scans, has found "previously undiscovered" levels of cognitive impairment in high school players who suffered no concussions. Researchers Eric Nauman, Thomas Talavage, and Larry Leverenz recorded up to 1,800 hits in a season, primarily among linemen and linebackers. G forces of the hits generally ranged from four times to more than 20 times that of a roller coaster. There were four recorded hits of nearly 300 G.

The number of hits correlates with the working assumption by BU researchers that high school football linemen likely absorb between 1,000 and 1,500 subconcussive head blows a season.

"We can see what part of the brain shuts down or works twice as hard to complete a task," Nauman said in an interview. "As these hits accumulate, different parts of the brain stop working, and other parts are being recruited to cover up for the damage. Even though they may not show symptoms, the brain has changed. We scratch our heads, both at what the brain can take and the damage the brain can hide."

In November, an Albert Einstein medical school study also found subconcussive trauma among adult men and women amateur soccer players who frequently headed the ball. In an amazing parallel to the estimated number of head hits to football linemen, significant trauma was seen in soccer players who headed the ball 1,000 to 1,500 times a season.

FAST FACT

In 2011 researchers at Boston University conservatively estimated that about 3.7 percent of all US professional football players have chronic traumatic encephalopathy.

"It only amounts to a few times a day for a regular player," said Einstein researcher Michael Lipton in a press release. "Heading a soccer ball is not an impact of a magnitude that will lacerate nerve fibers in the brain. But repetitive heading may set off a cascade of responses that can lead to degeneration of brain cells."

It is a cascade that, despite the publicity given to the NFL and the NHL, knows no gender. Purdue's Nauman said heading in girls has a g-force four to eight times that of a roller coaster, and can also cause cognitive impairment without an actual concussion. In a sports medicine journal review article last year, the BU researchers noted that the rate of concussion for collegiate women's soccer players is slightly higher than for male football players, the rate for women's hockey players is more than twice that of male hockey players, and the rate of women's lacrosse players is equal to the men.

Getting the Head Out of the Way

With scientific restraint, McKee, Cantu and Stern cautioned against panic. As sports fans, they are not at all interested in banning contact sports. They just want to get the head out of the way.

But that isn't happening. Despite the media spotlight on concussions, brain safety is so lightly regarded in daily life that 85 percent of high school youths told federal researchers in 2009 that they rarely or never wore a helmet while bicycle riding, a percentage unchanged from 10 years ago. That is surely why bicycling is the second-leading cause of emergency brain injury treatment for boys and girls of all ages, after football.

It all adds up to a major course correction for collision sports. Banning collision sports for youths under 14 makes good sense, as Cantu suggests, but there should also be a federal commission to find ways to get head trauma out of normal high school play. Given the up to 1,800 hits per year and the cautionary story of Owen Thomas, high school and youth football linemen should be held to a strict play count. With no new football helmet yet in sight that would prevent both skull fractures and concussions, it would mean re-teaching the techniques of tackling to end any leading with the head, launching off the feet, and helmet-to-helmet hits, even accidental ones.

In soccer, that means eliminating heading from high school on down and setting a maximum number of times a college player can head the ball in practice and in games. In hockey, that means banning all fighting and penalizing even accidental hits to the head. It means ending body checks that crush and rattle players against the boards.

It means the NFL, NHL, and Major League Soccer [MLS] must lead by example in making it clear that the brain comes before brutality. The NFL must end all launching of players, and penalize all helmet-to-helmet hits. The NHL must ban fighting and slamming against the boards. The MLS must set limits for heading.

Stern is often asked about NFL Hall of Fame quarterbacks Steve Young, 50, and Troy Aikman, 45, each of whom suffered many concussions, but now are both successful television football analysts.

"That's like saying, 'Here's a 60-year-old woman who doesn't have breast cancer, so how can you say that there's a risk of getting breast cancer?' It's really a ridiculous argument," Stern said.

More Research Is Needed

Yet to be done is research that better identifies concussions and subconcussive damage. Cantu said that for every recognized concussion, seven or eight are probably missed. The BU team has begun to interview 100 living former NFL players to explore possible treatments for CTE while athletes are alive. "We don't yet have therapies that get at the root of the underlying problem, because we don't really yet understand the problem," Cantu said.

" . . . We don't know how much impact is necessary, what are the genetic factors or the environmental factors such as how many blows close together or far apart does it take. What we do know scares us."

Couple that with McKee's belief that the data are "only going to get stronger." That should make the constellations of tau in her slides the center of the contact-sports universe, before another generation of pee-wee football, soccer, and hockey players enter this black hole.

Tommy John Surgery Has Saved Many Baseball Players' Careers

Will Carroll and Thomas Gorman

In the following article Will Carroll and Thomas Gorman discuss Tommy John surgery and the impact the procedure has had on the careers of many Major League Baseball pitchers. According to the authors, the mechanisms involved in overhand pitching are stressful to the elbow joint; in particular, causing damage to the ulnar collateral ligament (UCL). In 1974 a pitcher by the name of Tommy John was the first to undergo UCL replacement surgery. According to the authors, the procedure, which was coined "Tommy John surgery" by its inventor, has saved the careers of many major league pitchers and become an important part of baseball.

At the time this article was published, Carroll was a staff writer for *Baseball Prospectus*, an online publication that provides statistical and other types of analyses on baseball at baseballprospectus .com. Gorman is a San Francisco–based writer who often collaborated with Carroll on *Baseball Prospectus* articles.

Kerry Wood. Matt Morris. John Smoltz. Mariano Rivera. Tom Gordon. Eric Gagne. Other than an ability to throw a ball past the best hitters in the world, what these hurlers have in common is a four-inch scar on their pitching arm. They're not the only ones. *USA Today* reports that in the 2002 and 2003 seasons, 75 of the almost 700 pitchers who appeared in the majors were Tommy John surgery survivors. That's approximately one in every nine pitchers.

Tommy John surgery—technically, an ulnar collateral ligament replacement procedure—has saved the careers of hundreds of major league players. It may one day make the Hall of Fame case for its inventor, surgeon Frank Jobe (who was Hollywood enough to trademark the name "Tommy John procedure"). Thirty years after Jobe was told by his patient to "make something up," we take a closer look at the surgery that changed the game and some of the recent advancements that have made it such a medical wonder.

Anatomy of the Elbow

First some anatomy: the elbow is a hinge joint, moving in only one dimension (flex or extend), making it relatively simple from an architectural and functional standpoint. The humerus bone in the upper arm connects to the two bones of the forearm by means of various connective tissues. For a pitcher, one of the most important of these connections is the ulnar collateral ligament (UCL). The UCL offers much of the stability that is necessary for the elbow to withstand the extreme stresses created by throwing a baseball at high velocity. Its function is to stabilize against lateral forces and to keep the arm connected across the joint space.

Pitching overhand is a particularly stressful motion; the strain it puts on a player's joint is commonly injurious. Sometimes the UCL will weaken and stretch (technically a sprain), making it incompetent. Other times a catastrophic stress will cause the structure to "pop" or blow out. The injury isn't tremendously painful, and it can be incredibly difficult to diagnose without sophisticated imaging (such as an MRI [magnetic resonance imaging]), but incompetent or blown out, a damaged UCL will prevent a player from throwing at full velocity or with effective control.

Until recently, a UCL injury was career-ending or, at the very least, a major detour in a career path. Some believe that [pitching legend] Sandy Koufax's "dead arm" in 1966 was simply a case of a damaged UCL. It is unknown how many pitchers prior to 1974 could have benefited from this type of procedure, but given the rate of surgeries today and what we know about the workloads of the past, it is reasonable to assume that one out of every ten or so pitchers who burned out or simply faded away might have been saved.

Building a New Ligament

Crudely described, what Jobe did was build John a new ligament. Since no artificial tissue can fully approximate the function of the body's own connective tissues, and since the body doesn't have a whole lot of spare ligaments lying around, Jobe began by harvesting a healthy tendon. In most cases the tendon is harvested from the forearm of the patient, one attached to the Palmaris longus muscle. This tendon is not crucial for anatomical function, and in fact, 15 percent of people do not have the tendon. To see your palmaris longus tendon, look at the palmside of your forearm. Touch your thumb and little finger and then make as much of a fist as possible. Eighty-five percent of you should be able to see this tendon running down your arm.

San Francisco Giants team orthopedist Ken Akizuki reports that when the palmaris longus tendon is unavailable, the surgeon will often use the plantaris tendon in the ankle or a small part of the hamstring tendon in the leg. Usually this tendon will be harvested from the leg that is not used as the plant foot in the pitcher's delivery. The removal of either of these tendons has a negligible effect on function.

Next, the surgeon has to open up the elbow. In the original procedure, Frank Jobe used a large incision to get exposure to the joint. For an idea of the size of this incision, hold your right arm out from your body with your palm pointed upwards. With your other hand, feel along the inside of the elbow until you can find what feels like a hard round nub. That's the proximal end of your ulna bone. The incision would have taken place along the inside of the arm, beginning several inches above the elbow and ending several inches below.

More recently, [former major league pitcher] Kris Benson used his Web cam to document the healing of his own Tommy John scar. In the first image you can actually see the two incisions in his forearm that were used to remove his palmaris longus tendon. Benson's elbow incision is quite a bit smaller than the scars left by early Tommy John procedures.

As Dr. Akizuki explains, "In order to get exposure to the joint you used to have to detach the entire flexor attachment [the muscles that flex the elbow—you can feel those muscles by feeling along the incision site]. You used to just fillet that open."

Once inside the elbow the ulnar nerve is recognized, lifted out, and moved to provide greater access to the joint. This is the "funny bone" nerve and it runs inside the ulnar groove.

Dr. Tim Kremchek, Medical Director of the Cincinnati Reds and one of the four doctors who do most of the Tommy John surgeries on major league pitchers, explains that in early versions of the procedure this was a problematic part of the surgery. "Sometimes the movement of the nerve would cause scarring and you would need to go back in and re-release it." This was the case for Tommy

A baseball pitcher shows his scar from Tommy John surgery, a procedure first used successfully on all-star major league pitcher Tommy John in 1974. The procedure remedies injury to the ulnar collateral ligament (UCL) in the elbow. (© AP Images/ The Daily Reflector, Greg Eans)

John. A second procedure to correct his nerve problems guaranteed that his DL [disabled list] stint would last the entire 1975 season.

With the muscle separated and the ulnar nerve safely out of the way, the surgeon would then locate the damaged ligament. After scraping out the damaged tissue, the next step is to drill tunnels in the elbow. If you were imagining a Makita [drill] with a quarter-inch bit you wouldn't be too far off. Two different drill passes are made through the humerus in a V-shape aimed at the ulna, and one more tunnel runs through the ulna at approximately a perpendicular angle to the humerus. The result is a pattern that allows for the surgeon to loop the harvested tendon through the various holes in a series of figure-eight patterns.

Over time, the transplanted tendon "ligamentizes," which basically means it learns to become a ligament. There is a healthy blood supply from the muscle above the surgery site (the one the surgeon had to cut through), and there is also a hope that the drilling will give the harvested tendon access to the vascular [blood vessel] supply of the humerus and ulna. It is not completely clear how it is that a tendon becomes a ligament, although Dr. Akizuki thinks that range of motion exercises help the tendon learn that it is being used as a ligament now and that it needs to adapt. Surgeons don't go back in to biopsy the repaired elbow to see how the tissue has changed, but follow-up MRIs do show that the new tissue is maturing and functioning as a ligament should.

That's basically it. Or at least, that would be it if surgeons and trainers and pitching coaches and GMs [team general managers] weren't a tinkering sort and didn't try to keep one-upping each other.

Improvements to the Technique

Dr. Kremchek, who does some 120 UCL replacements a year, detailed some of the many improvements in the surgical technique that have been made since the original procedure. After noting that the drill equipment they use is more sophisticated, he explained, "the entire procedure is less invasive. We leave the ulnar nerve, and we leave the damaged ligament."

Making the procedure less invasive isn't about having a smaller, prettier scar; it's about doing as little damage as possible to the surrounding muscles and tissues. Leaving the ulnar nerve in place reduces the risk of scarring or permanent nerve damage. Scarring would require a second procedure to re-release the nerve, whereas nerve damage could leave a pitcher with permanent numbness or tingling in part of the hand, a condition that would make pitching tricky.

Leaving the damaged ligament in place can help in a couple of ways. First, like any ligament, the UCL has nerve receptors. These receptors allow for proprioception, which is a fancy name for the body's ability to sense the position, location, orientation and movement of its parts. If you close your eyes, you can still tell what position your body is in due to proprioception. A damaged ligament can no longer serve its stabilizing function, but its nerve receptors can still contribute to the elbow joint's combined ability for proprioception. If the damaged ligament is removed completely, the new ligament must develop its own proprioception, a long and complicated process that physicians don't completely understand.

Another reason for leaving the damaged ligament in place is that the structural attachments of the old ligament are still there. As Dr. Akizuki explained, "If you look at a biomechanics study, the number of loops you put in is not as important as fixation at each end." Dr. Akizuki detailed the way he uses the old ligament structures: "I split the old ligament longitudinally [lengthwise], peel it open from top and bottom—the attachments at the top and bottom are still intact, even though they might be loose. I free it up distally and proximally [at both ends], pass the new ligament across and suture it. The priority is on the new ligament first. You may have to debride [scrape] out some of the old ligament but if it's just loose you can overlap it."

No one is exactly sure whether the proprioception advantage or the structural advantage is more important. What the surgeons do know, though, is that leaving in the damaged ligament doesn't make the procedure any harder. After leaving the damaged ligament in place, what some have called an "overlay Tommy John," the cutting edge is probably the use of bio-absorbable screws instead of drilling tunnels through the bone for attaching the harvested tendon, but the use of such screws is still experimental.

The Importance of Post-Surgical Rehab

Yet Dr. Kremchek is adamant that we understand that surgery is not the most important part of the equation. In fact, he says that post-surgical rehab makes up at least

55% of the solution for an elbow injury and that the "difference maker is the rehab people, not the surgeon." Shocking words from a man whose profession is not well known for deferring credit or modesty.

Kremchek explains, "The crucial element is communication between the surgeon, therapist, trainer and pitching coach. When you diagnose a UCL injury you don't want to waste a ton of time with the rehab. Go straight into surgery." *BP*'s [*Baseball Prospectus*'s] Injury Database concurs. Surgery produces a much higher success rate than just straight rehab. "Keep the communication lines open. Everyone gets my cell phone number: players, agents, coaches, GMs. Progress safely and if everything falls into place, these ultra-fast returns are possible."

As a case study, consider Ryan Dempster. Dempster was placed on the DL on August 1, 2003, a Friday, and on the following Monday he was under Dr. Tim Kremchek's knife in Cincinnati. The Reds released Dempster in November; by January his agent was talking with the Chicago Cubs.

Cubs GM Jim Hendry was involved in negotiations with Jon Lieber before [New York Yankees owner] George Steinbrenner's pocketbook knocked him out of the picture, so the idea of signing a pitcher with a serious arm injury was not completely foreign. As Hendry explained it, "We had a good relationship with Dr. Kremchek. We've had him look at our guys before. Our staff liked him. We called him in the past for other players and our medical team thought his diagnosis was dead on. I don't think we assumed a lot of risk. We felt comfortable with our talks with Dr. Kremchek. We felt Dempster was on or ahead of schedule in the winter."

All throughout Dempster's rehab, Dr. Kremchek was in constant communication both with Dempster and with Larry Rothschild, the Cubs pitching coach who was helping

> **FAST FACT**
>
> A review of the effectiveness of Tommy John surgery published in the *American Journal of Sports Medicine* in 2008 found that, overall, 83 percent of patients had an "excellent result."

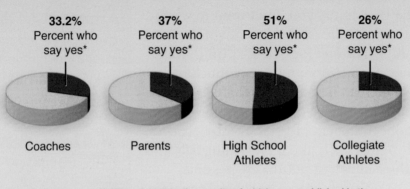

Tommy John Surgery for Performance Enhancement

Question: "Should Tommy John surgery be performed on players without elbow surgery to enhance performance?"

33.2%	**37%**	**51%**	**26%**
Percent who say yes*	Percent who say yes*	Percent who say yes*	Percent who say yes*
Coaches	Parents	High School Athletes	Collegiate Athletes

*Based on a survey of 260 participants, the results of which were published in the May 2012 edition of *The Physician and Sports Medicine*.

Taken from: Christopher S. Ahmed, et al. "Public Perceptions of Tommy John Surgery." *The Physician and Sports Medicine*, May 2012.

to manage Dempster's progress. Available by cell phone, Kremchek could help the team make quick decisions about advancing the hard-tossing righty. Dempster was throwing in extended Spring Training and Class A ball in May; he was in Triple-A in June and July; and on August 1, exactly a year to the day from when he was first put on the DL, he was called up to the Cubs' 25-man roster.

Hendry, for one, says he wouldn't be surprised to see more and more teams regularly signing guys with elbow injuries. "Our situation in our minor league system is that we've had a lot of success with rehab from elbow surgeries."

Successful by Any Measure

There are always surgeons working on more advances as well. Several teams are working on techniques that would

PERSPECTIVES ON DISEASES AND DISORDERS

allow the operation to be performed arthroscopically [using a thin scope rather than cutting open the whole arm], reducing the stress on the arm. There are amazing advances in the rehabilitation process, most notably by Kevin Wilk and his team from ASMI [American Sports Medicine Institute]. Even the material used is being reconsidered with "cloned" ligaments, built from stem cells and grown in a dish being considered as an alternative to the harvested tendons used today.

That Tommy John surgery seems all too common is perhaps the best measure of its success. While there is still a failure rate of 10 to 15 percent, most of these happen on younger subjects. It would be more accurate to say that the pitcher fails himself in most cases, rather than the surgery being the problem. Some think the procedure is becoming too common, with younger and younger patients. Others want to have their "prospect" son given the procedure when young so as to avoid it later.

While there are faults, the surgery and the team behind the procedures have made baseball better. One in nine pitchers would not be on the field without it, further diluting the pitching population. Frank Jobe's experiment on a desperate pitcher has become a part of America's game, a routine procedure taken for granted. That alone is pretty amazing.

How Sports Injuries Are Treated

National Institute of Arthritis and Musculoskeletal and Skin Disease

In the following article the National Institute of Arthritis and Musculoskeletal and Skin Diseases (NIAMS) discusses the treatment of sports injuries. According to NIAMS, many sports injuries can be treated at home using the RICE regimen, which includes rest, ice, compression, and elevation; however, notes NIAMS, some sports-related injuries are more severe and may require surgery. According to the author, after suffering an injury, most injured athletes require rehabilitation, or a graduated exercise program, in order to return to playing sports.

NIAMS is a branch of the National Institutes of Health and is focused on supporting research into the causes, treatment, and prevention of arthritis and musculoskeletal and skin diseases.

W hether an injury is acute or chronic, there is never a good reason to try to "work through" the pain of an injury. When you have pain from a particular movement or activity, STOP! Continuing the activity only causes further harm.

Some injuries require prompt medical attention . . . , while others can be self-treated. Here's what you need to know about both types:

When to Seek Medical Treatment and When to Treat at Home

You should call a health professional if:

- The injury causes severe pain, swelling, or numbness.
- You can't tolerate any weight on the area.
- The pain or dull ache of an old injury is accompanied by increased swelling or joint abnormality or instability. . . .

If you don't have any of the above symptoms, it's probably safe to treat the injury at home—at least at first. If pain or other symptoms worsen, it's best to check with your health care provider. Use the RICE method to relieve pain and inflammation and speed healing. Follow these four steps immediately after injury and continue for at least 48 hours.

- *Rest.* Reduce regular exercise or activities of daily living as needed. If you cannot put weight on an ankle or knee, crutches may help. If you use a cane or one crutch for an ankle injury, use it on the uninjured side to help you lean away and relieve weight on the injured ankle.
- *Ice.* Apply an ice pack to the injured area for 20 minutes at a time, four to eight times a day. A cold pack, ice bag, or plastic bag filled with crushed ice

and wrapped in a towel can be used. To avoid cold injury and frostbite, do not apply the ice for more than 20 minutes. (Note: Do not use heat immediately after an injury. This tends to increase internal bleeding or swelling. Heat can be used later on to relieve muscle tension and promote relaxation.)

- *Compression.* Compression of the injured area may help reduce swelling. Compression can be achieved with elastic wraps, special boots, air casts, and splints. Ask your health care provider for advice on which one to use.
- *Elevation.* If possible, keep the injured ankle, knee, elbow, or wrist elevated on a pillow, above the level of the heart, to help decrease swelling. . . .

Whom Should I See for My Injury?

Although severe injuries will need to be seen immediately in an emergency room, particularly if they occur on the weekend or after office hours, most sports injuries can be evaluated and, in many cases, treated by your primary health care provider.

Depending on your preference and the severity of your injury or the likelihood that your injury may cause ongoing, long-term problems, you may want to see, or have your primary health care professional refer you to, one of the following:

- *Orthopaedic surgeon:* A doctor specializing in the diagnosis and treatment of the musculoskeletal system, which includes bones, joints, ligaments, tendons, muscles, and nerves.
- *Physical therapist/physiotherapist:* A health care professional who can develop a rehabilitation program. Your primary care physician may refer you to a physical therapist after you begin to recover from your injury to help strengthen muscles and joints and prevent further injury.

How Are Sports Injuries Treated?

Although using the RICE technique described previously can be helpful for any sports injury, RICE is often just a starting point. Here are some other treatments your doctor or other health care provider may administer, recommend, or prescribe to help your injury heal.

Nonsteroidal Anti-inflammatory Drugs (NSAIDs)

The moment you are injured, chemicals are released from damaged tissue cells. This triggers the first stage of healing: inflammation. . . . Inflammation causes tissues to become swollen, tender, and painful. Although inflammation is needed for healing, it can actually slow the healing process if left unchecked.

To reduce inflammation and pain, doctors and other health care providers often recommend taking an over-the-counter (OTC) nonsteroidal anti-inflammatory drug (NSAID) such as aspirin, ibuprofen . . . , ketoprofen . . . , or naproxen sodium. . . . For more severe pain and inflammation, doctors may prescribe one of several dozen NSAIDs available in prescription strength. . . .

Though not an NSAID, another commonly used OTC medication, acetaminophen (Tylenol), may relieve pain. It has no effect on inflammation, however.

FAST FACT

According to the National Athletic Trainers' Association, more than half of all sports injuries occur during practice.

Immobilization and Surgery

Immobilization is a common treatment for sports injuries that may be done immediately by a trainer or paramedic. Immobilization involves reducing movement in the area to prevent further damage. By enabling the blood supply to flow more directly to the injury (or the site of surgery to repair damage from an injury), immobilization reduces pain, swelling, and muscle spasm and helps the healing process begin. Following are some devices used for immobilization:

- Slings immobilize the upper body, including the arms and shoulders.
- Splints and casts to support and protect injured bones and soft tissue. Casts can be made from plaster or fiberglass. Splints can be custom made or ready made. Standard splints come in a variety of shapes and sizes and have Velcro straps that make them easy to put on and take off or adjust. Splints generally offer less support and protection than a cast, and therefore may not always be a treatment option.
- Leg immobilizers to keep the knee from bending after injury or surgery. Made from foam rubber covered with fabric, leg immobilizers enclose the entire leg, fastening with Velcro straps.

In some cases, surgery is needed to repair torn connective tissues or to realign bones with compound fractures. The vast majority of sports injuries, however, do not require surgery.

Rehabilitation (Exercise) and Rest

A key part of rehabilitation from sports injuries is a graduated exercise program designed to return the injured body part to a normal level of function.

With most injuries, early mobilization—getting the part moving as soon as possible—will speed healing. Generally, early mobilization starts with gentle range-of-motion exercises and then moves on to stretching and strengthening exercise when you can [do these] without increasing pain. For example, if you have a sprained ankle, you may be able to work on range of motion for the first day or two after the sprain by gently tracing letters with your big toe. Once your range of motion is fairly good, you can start doing gentle stretching and strengthening exercises. When you are ready, weights may be added to your exercise routine to further strengthen the injured area. The key is to avoid movement that causes pain.

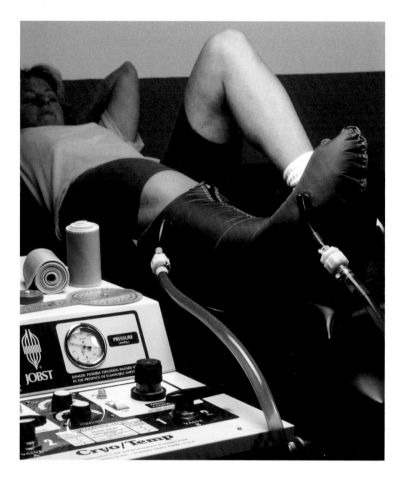

After suffering an injury, most athletes require rehabilitation with a graduated therapeutic exercise program in order to return to playing. (© Mira/Alamy)

As damaged tissue heals, scar tissue forms, which shrinks and brings torn or separated tissues back together. As a result, the injury site becomes tight or stiff, and damaged tissues are at risk of reinjury. That's why stretching and strengthening exercises are so important. You should continue to stretch the muscles daily and as the first part of your warmup before exercising.

When planning your rehabilitation program with a health care professional, remember that progression is the key principle. Start with just a few exercises, do them often, and then gradually increase how much you do. A complete rehabilitation program should include exercises for flexibility, endurance, and strength; instruction in

Knee Injuries Are the Most Common Sports-Related Injury Requiring Surgery

Most Commonly Injured Body Sites Requiring Surgery*

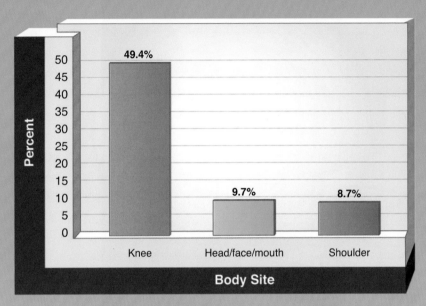

*Among American high school athletes from 2005 to 2010.

Taken from: J.A. Rechel, C.L. Collins, and R.D. Comstock. "Epidemiology of Injuries Requiring Surgery Among High School Athletes in United States, 2005–2010." *Journal of Trauma*, October 2011.

balance and proper body mechanics related to the sport; and a planned return to full participation.

Throughout the rehabilitation process, avoid painful activities and concentrate on those exercises that will improve function in the injured part. Don't resume your sport until you are sure you can stretch the injured tissues without any pain, swelling, or restricted movement, and monitor any other symptoms. When you do return to your sport, start slowly and gradually build up to full participation. . . .

Although it is important to get moving as soon as possible, you must also take time to rest following an injury. All injuries need time to heal; proper rest will help the process. Your health care professional can guide you regarding the proper balance between rest and rehabilitation.

Other Therapies

Other therapies commonly used in rehabilitating sports injuries include:

- *Electrostimulation:* Mild electrical current provides pain relief by preventing nerve cells from sending pain impulses to the brain. Electrostimulation may also be used to decrease swelling, and to make muscles in immobilized limbs contract, thus preventing muscle atrophy and maintaining or increasing muscle strength.
- *Cold/cryotherapy:* Ice packs reduce inflammation by constricting blood vessels and limiting blood flow to the injured tissues. Cryotherapy eases pain by numbing the injured area. It is generally used for only the first 48 hours after injury.
- *Heat/thermotherapy:* Heat, in the form of hot compresses, heat lamps, or heating pads, causes the blood vessels to dilate and increase blood flow to the injury site. Increased blood flow aids the healing process by removing cell debris from damaged tissues and carrying healing nutrients to the injury site. Heat also helps to reduce pain. It should not be applied within the first 48 hours after an injury.
- *Ultrasound:* High-frequency sound waves produce deep heat that is applied directly to an injured area. Ultrasound stimulates blood flow to promote healing.
- *Massage:* Manual pressing, rubbing, and manipulation soothe tense muscles and increase blood flow to the injury site.

Most of these therapies are administered or supervised by a licensed health care professional.

Athletes Look to Biologic Medicine to Treat Sports Injuries

Nicholas Kulish

In the following article Nicholas Kulish examines an alternative treatment for sports injuries that is drawing many injured American athletes to Germany to undergo the treatment. Called Regenokine therapy, the treatment is based on extracting, manipulating, and then reinjecting anti-inflammatory proteins from a sample of the athlete's own blood. This approach of using a patient's own tissues to treat injuries is a type of treatment known as "biologic medicine." Regenokine therapy is not yet approved for use in the United States and has not been scientifically validated, notes Kulish; however, many athletes, including Los Angeles Lakers basketball star Kobe Bryant, are convinced of the therapy's benefits and offer praise for its inventor.

Kulish is a *New York Times* journalist based in Germany.

The medical treatment for Lindsey Berg's arthritic left knee has not been approved by the Food and Drug Administration (FDA), and neither her professional volleyball team in Italy nor the United States Olympic team would help with the cost. But for Berg, a gold medal hopeful, the chance to dull the chronic pain was worth the money, and the risk.

So between the end of her professional season and the start of Olympic practices in California, Berg stopped at the office of Dr. Peter Wehling on the bank of the Rhine River [in Germany]. "I've been struggling with knee pain for the last four years and just continuing to play on it," said Berg, 31, who had tried surgery and cortisone injections to little avail.

A Pilgrimage for Athletes

After examining her, Wehling and his team drew syringes of her blood. First they incubated it. Then they spun it in a centrifuge. The blood cells produce proteins that reduce inflammation and stimulate cellular growth; sometimes additional anti-inflammatory proteins are added to the solution. Finally, Wehling injected the orange serum into Berg's knee.

The price came to 6,000 euros, or about $7,400, out of her own pocket, but with the Olympics in London coming up, any treatment that might make her knee better was worth it. "It's your body and your money because they're not paying for it," she said with cheerful resignation, on the fourth day of her treatment.

Wehling's practice has become almost a pilgrimage site for athletes trying to prolong careers that have tested the limits of their bodies. It has also been the subject of no small amount of speculation after word leaked last year [2011] that the Los Angeles Lakers star Kobe Bryant had flown to Düsseldorf [Germany] for the treatments. Alex Rodriguez of the Yankees traveled there as well. After the N.B.A. [National Basketball Association] season ended, Lakers center Andrew Bynum, Bryant's teammate, said he, too, would try it.

Commentators wanted to know if there was something fishy that required Bryant to go abroad for medical treatment. As his scoring average increased and the aging star seemed rejuvenated, the interest in the trips to Germany and the unusual treatment grew.

To answer the most common questions: Wehling's practice is not at the end of a dark alley but in a modern building south of the city's old town; it is brightly rather than dimly lighted, with orange floors and a water cooler in the waiting room; and Wehling seems more like a true believer in his Regenokine therapy than a snake-oil salesman. He said he was careful not to use any substances banned by athletic governing bodies.

Using Biology to Treat Sports Injuries

Biologic medicine is a rapidly growing field. Wehling's Regenokine treatment might sound similar to another blood-spinning treatment, known as platelet-rich plasma, or P.R.P., that has gained popularity in the United States in recent years. In that procedure, the goal is to produce a high concentration of platelet cells, which are believed to speed the healing process. Wehling said his treatment differed from P.R.P. because he heats the blood before it is spun to increase the concentration of anti-inflammatory proteins, rather than the platelets, in his cell-free solution.

The idea is not just to focus on mechanical problems in the joints or lower back but to treat inflammation as a cause of tissue damage as well as a symptom.

"The potential of biology to treat orthopedic problems is high because it has only been developed a little," Wehling said in an interview.

"It has to be embedded in a good concept more broadly," he added, emphasizing that sleep, diet and conditioning are among the important components to go with the injections. "There's no such thing as the one therapy that fixes everything."

On a recent morning he treated not only Berg but also a basketball player, a golfer, a Hollywood executive and a former martial artist.

FAST FACT

Regenokine therapy costs about six hundred to fifteen hundred dollars per shot per joint (patients generally need two shots per week per joint), according to the therapy's developer, Dr. Peter Wehling.

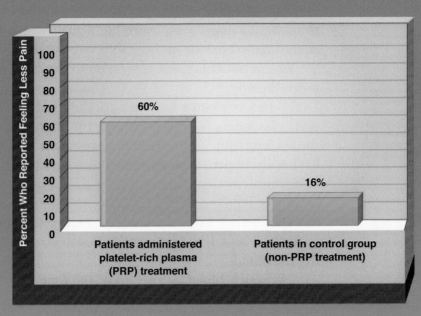

Biologic Medicine Treatment Helps Ease Pain of Tennis Elbow

Percent Who Reported Feeling Less Pain

60%

16%

Patients administered
platelet-rich plasma
(PRP) treatment

Patients in control group
(non-PRP treatment)

*Based on a study of 140 patients, surveyed eight weeks after treatment.

Taken from: A. Mishra and T. Pavelko. "Treatment of Chronic Elbow Tendinosis with Buffered Platelet-Rich Plasma." *American Journal of Sports Medicine*, November 2006.

"The results were incredible," Vijay Singh, the world's former No. 1 golfer and a patient of Wehling's, said in a telephone interview. "It's like somebody just put oil all over your body. It lubes you up, and you're able to move more freely, especially pain free."

The question is how effective the treatment will prove in the long run.

Dr. Freddie Fu, a professor of orthopedic surgery at the University of Pittsburgh, has been critical of many such treatments, including P.R.P. He was slightly more optimistic about Wehling's approach.

"The gimmick is, it's your own body, it must be safe," Fu said. "There has been some impressive research done already, and there is a good scientific fundament to do more research.

"However, before the F.D.A. [US Food and Drug Administration] approves, more high-quality independent trials have to be done in order to prove the effectiveness."

Recent patients speak glowingly of the doctor as well as his therapy.

"When you come here and are skeptical and all your pain disappears, it makes you all the more devoted to the science of it," said Tim Shaheen, from Los Angeles. "What about people on assembly lines with terrible knees and terrible backs? This would be a lifesaver for that in quality of life."

The therapy generally lasts five days, starting with an evaluation and, if the patient decides to go ahead, drawing the blood.

"As much blood as they took the first day, I didn't think I'd have any left," said Wes Short Jr., a professional golfer from Austin, Tex. It was his first trip to Germany, he said, indeed his first to a non-English-speaking country, and he still marveled at the fact that most of the taxis were Mercedeses.

Short lay on his stomach, his green short-sleeve shirt hiked up. Wehling had just injected several syringes of serum into the small of his back. Afterward the doctor left half a dozen acupuncture needles quivering in Short's back.

The fact that Wehling had treated Pope John Paul II made a strong impression on Short. "I'm sure he [the former pope] doesn't trust just anybody," said Short, who hoped to start playing again if the treatment worked.

Bedside Manner

Wehling's book *The End of Pain* begins with a *Da Vinci Code*–style trip to the Vatican and, escorted by the Swiss Guard, into John Paul II's private chamber. "The hard marble floors echoed with emptiness," Wehling wrote.

Dr. Peter Wehling treated US volleyball gold medalist Lindsey Berg with Regenokine therapy. The therapy entails extracting, manipulating, and then reinjecting anti-inflammatory proteins from a sample of the athlete's blood. (© **AP Images/Jeff Roberson**)

But why, he asked, had the pope chosen his treatment? "Because your treatment comes from God," the pope said, referring, Wehling wrote, to the fact that it comes from the body.

Wehling comes from an old Rhineland family. His great-uncle was the archbishop of Cologne, and as a boy he met the future Pope Benedict XVI, Joseph Ratzinger. A father of two, Wehling plays keyboard in two bands, one jazz and one blues, giving off the vibe of a goofy-cool uncle, a little too enthusiastic to be completely hip.

"He's very honest," said Jeff Kwatinetz, president of the production company Prospect Park, who traveled from Los Angeles to receive the treatment on both shoulders. He was as impressed with Wehling's bedside manner as the mobility he had regained in his joints. "He hopes it can work, thinks it can work, but he's not making any promises."

Wehling manages to buzz through his clinic at high speed yet somehow make each patient feel as though he has all the time in the world for him or her. When talking to Wehling, the term "exciting," is often used—the research, the possibilities. There are two offices, one in New York and one in Los Angeles, licensed to provide a similar treatment, though they cannot advertise because of the lack of F.D.A. approval.

"When you're one of the progenitors of a new way of thinking, you really want to have it thrive," said Chris Evans, the Müller Professor of Orthopedic Surgery at Harvard Medical School, who wrote the introduction to Wehling's book and serves unpaid on the supervisory board of the company Wehling founded. He is developing an idea that came to him when he was a young resident in neurophysiology and orthopedics, Dr. Evans said, and "now that he's middle-aged he wants to see that it's out there and that it works."

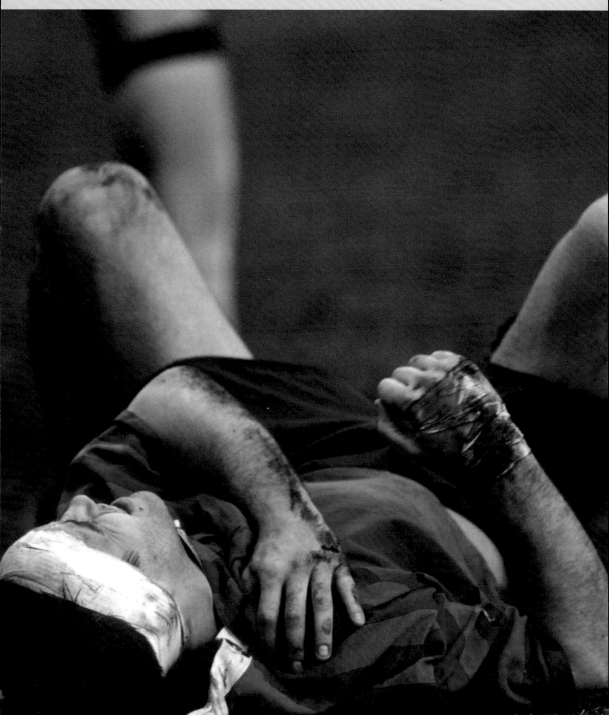

CHAPTER 2

Controversies About Sports Injuries

There Is an Epidemic of Youth Sports Injuries Caused by Overplaying

Jane E. Brody

In the following viewpoint Jane E. Brody, the Personal Health columnist for the *New York Times*, asserts that a growing number of children are suffering sports-related injuries, particularly those caused when a joint or muscle is overused. Brody attributes much of the problem to kids' playing one sport all year round and not giving their bodies a chance to recover. Brody also blames the rise in these injuries on a youth sports culture in which kids are pushed to compete in hopes that they might someday be professional athletes. Yet, says Brody, few kids ever end up playing professional sports.

Photo on previous page. A rugby player lies injured on the field. Sports injuries and their treatment and prevention have recently become a source of public controversy. (© PCN Photography/ Alamy)

I'd be the last person to discourage children from playing sports. Indeed, I wish many more would move away from their computers, put down their iPods and cellphones and devote more time and energy to physical activities.

But for many children and adolescents, the problem is the opposite of being sedentary. Encouraged by par-

SOURCE: Jane E. Brody, "For Children in Sports, a Breaking Point," DrAxe.com, May 24, 2010. www.draxe.com. Copyright © 2010 by DrAxe.com. All rights reserved. Reproduced by permission.

ents and coaches, many with visions of glory and scholarships, too many young athletes are being pushed—or are pushing themselves—to the point of breaking down, physically and sometimes emotionally.

The statistics cited by Mark Hyman in his book *Until It Hurts: America's Obsession with Youth Sports and How It Harms Our Kids*, are sobering indeed: "Every year more than 3.5 million children under 15 require medical treatment for sports injuries, nearly half of which are the result of simple overuse."

Injuries are only part of the problem, Mr. Hyman wrote. As adults become more and more involved, he noted, "with each passing season youth sports seem to stray further and further from its core mission of providing healthy, safe and character-building recreation for children."

Mr. Hyman, a sports journalist, was prompted to tackle this subject in part by his own misguided behavior as the father of an athletically talented son. At 13, Ben Hyman was a prized pitcher for a local team when his shoulder began to hurt—and hurt enough for him to complain—just before the start of league playoffs.

Despite a professional assessment that Ben's problem was caused by throwing too many baseballs and a recommendation to rest his arm up to a month, his father put him in the game, and again three days later, urging him to "blaze a trail to the championship." When the injured boy began "lamely lobbing balls at home plate," Mr. Hyman realized his foolish shortsightedness in putting winning ahead of his son's well-being.

The Dangers of Overdoing It

The problem was put into focus three years ago [in 2007] by the American Academy of Pediatrics' Council on Sports Medicine and Fitness. In a report in the academy's journal, *Pediatrics*, Dr. Joel S. Brenner wrote, "Overuse injuries, overtraining and burnout among child and adolescent athletes are a growing problem in the United States."

The goal of youth participation in sports, the council said, "should be to promote lifelong physical activity, recreation and skills of healthy competition."

"Unfortunately," it went on, "too often the goal is skewed toward adult (parent/coach) goals either implic-

Every year more than 3.5 million children under the age of fifteen require medical treatment for sports injuries, nearly half of which are the result of simply overusing a body part. (© **BSIP SA/ Alamy**)

PERSPECTIVES ON DISEASES AND DISORDERS

itly or explicitly. As more young athletes are becoming professionals at a younger age, there is more pressure to grab a piece of the 'professional pie,' to obtain a college scholarship or to make the Olympic team."

(If you doubt the role of adults, I suggest you take in a Little League game between teams striving for a championship. But instead of watching the players, watch—and listen to—the parents and coaches screaming at them, and not just words of encouragement.)

But most young athletes and their parents fail to realize that depending on the sport, only a tiny few—2 to 5 out of 1,000 high school athletes—ever achieve professional status.

Clearly we've gone too far when the emphasis on athletic participation and performance becomes all-consuming and causes injuries that can sometimes compromise a child's future.

The sports surgeon Dr. James R. Andrews said that he now sees four times as many overuse injuries in youth sports as he did just five years ago [in 2005] and that more children today are having to undergo surgery for chronic sports injuries.

> **FAST FACT**
>
> Overuse injury, which occurs over time from repeated motion, is responsible for nearly half of all sports injuries to middle and high school students, according to the National Center for Sports Safety.

Though far more common today, the problem is not new. In 1952, the National Education Association took aim at the "high-pressure elements" and "highly organized competition" in youth sports that gave youngsters "an exaggerated idea of the importance of sports and may even be harmful to them."

In 1988 in *The Archives of Disease in Childhood*, two London-based physicians, N. Maffulli and P. Helms, concluded, "Young athletes are not just smaller athletes, and they should not become sacrificial lambs to a coach's or parent's ego."

They cited an analysis of training regimens finding that "at least 60 percent of all injuries sustained were in direct relation to training and could be avoided by appropriate changes in training programs." They explained that young athletes are more prone to certain injuries, especially stress fractures; tendinitis; a degenerative condition called osteochondrosis; and damage to the growth plates of bones that can stunt them for life.

Whitney Phelps, the older sister of the Olympics wunderkind Michael Phelps, was the swimmer to watch in the 1990s, until she burned out her body. Motivated by her mother, her coach and her own dreams of the Olympics, she recalls, she swam through pain in her back for years, pain sometimes so severe she could hardly stand up. At 14, Mr. Hyman recounts in his book, her arms would go numb when she turned her head, and she was found to have two bulging spinal discs, a herniated disc and two stress fractures.

Playing It Safe

A major factor in the rising injury rate is the current emphasis on playing one sport all year long, which leaves no time for muscles and joints to recover from the inevitable microtrauma that occurs during practice and play. With increased specialization, there is also no cross-training that would enable other muscles to strengthen and lighten the load.

Even when a sport is done seasonally, daily practice can result in problems. The pediatrics council recommends that young athletes "have at least one to two days off per week from competitive athletics, sport-specific training and competitive practice (scrimmage) to allow them to recover both physically and psychologically." The group also recommends that children and adolescents play on only one team a season and take a vacation of two or three months from a specific sport each year.

Whatever an athlete's age, playing through pain is a bad idea. Pain is the body's signal that something is awry. Ignore it and it is likely to get worse and worse, and the injury could become permanent. Get a professional diag-

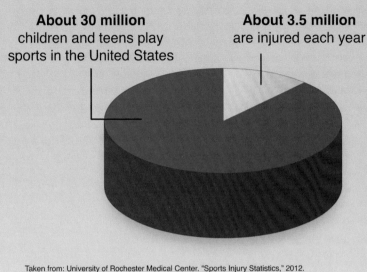

More than 10 Percent of Kids Who Play Sports Get Injured

About 30 million children and teens play sports in the United States

About 3.5 million are injured each year

Taken from: University of Rochester Medical Center. "Sports Injury Statistics," 2012. www.urmc.rochester.edu.

nosis and follow the therapeutic advice. After a prescribed period of rest, return gradually to the sport, increasing training time, repetitions or distance by no more than 10 percent each week.

The *Pediatrics* authors also suggest that it is a sign of possible burnout when an athlete "complains of nonspecific muscle or joint problems, fatigue or poor academic performance." That's when a child's motivation to continue in the sport should be reassessed.

There Is a Troubling Rise in Sports-Related Youth Concussions

Kathleen Doheny

Pediatricians have noted a significant increase in the number of children suffering concussions from sports activities, says Kathleen Doheny in the following selection. According to Doheny, about a quarter of a million American children visited a hospital emergency department for a sports-related concussion from 2001 to 2005. The number of actual concussions is likely even higher, contends Doheny, as many children do not visit the hospital but instead go directly to their pediatrician.

Doheny is a journalist specializing in health, fitness, and behavioral topics. In addition to *HealthDay,* she has written for WebMD, *Prevention,* and *Shape*, among others.

High school–age athletes are more likely than younger kids to have sports-related concussions, but the rate of such injuries in both groups is on the rise, a new U.S. study suggests.

From 1997 to 2007, emergency department visits for concussion in kids aged 8 to 13 playing organized sports doubled, and the number of visits increased by more than 200 percent in older teens, according to the report.

In related news, the American Academy of Pediatrics [AAP] has issued new guidelines on what to do about sports-related concussions, with advice for both parents and physicians. . . .

The study and guidelines are published online and in the September [2010] print issue of *Pediatrics*.

Awareness of concussions is increasing, according to Dr. Mark Halstead, who co-wrote the new recommendations. Unlike the thinking of a generation ago, concussions aren't something to "shake off," said Halstead, an assistant professor of pediatrics and orthopaedics at Washington University School of Medicine in St. Louis.

"A concussion is an injury to the brain that is typically not a structural injury but a functional injury," he explained. He tells parents to think of it as a computer bug. "If a computer gets a virus, the computer doesn't function appropriately."

Rest Is the Only "Medicine" That Works for a Concussion

Parents should know that "no athlete should go back to play on the same day they have their concussion. We recommend athletes who have a concussion be evaluated by a medical professional before they return to play," Halstead said.

There is no medication or treatment proven for concussion, other than rest, he added. That means resting the body and the brain, he noted.

Even homework, television and video games may worsen symptoms after a concussion, according to the AAP guidelines, which say that the young athlete may require a temporary leave of absence from school. The child should also be restricted from physical activity until there are no symptoms at rest or during exercise, the guidelines note.

Symptoms of a concussion generally resolve within about seven to 10 days, according to the AAP, but parents should seek additional medical help if symptoms worsen.

"Worrisome signs for us are a progressively increasing headache, if a child is unable to move an arm or leg, worsening symptoms, repeated throwing up," said Halstead. "Those are things that should be evaluated sooner." Other symptoms include feeling lightheaded or confused or losing consciousness.

The guidelines also suggest that retirement from contact sports should be considered for an athlete who has had multiple concussions or who has suffered post-concussion symptoms for more than three months.

FAST FACT

Boys' high school football had the highest overall rate of concussions at 6.94 per 10,000 athletes participating in school-sponsored practice or competition from 2008 to 2011, according to data from Ohio State University.

Which sports are riskiest for concussions? For organized team sports, concussions were most likely in football, as well as basketball, soccer and ice hockey; for individual and leisure sports, concussions were more likely during bicycling, playground games and snow skiing, the researchers found. To reduce injuries, the AAP recommends taking preventive steps, such as using protective equipment and padding goalposts.

From 2001 to 2005, there were an estimated 502,000 emergency department visits for concussion among U.S. kids aged 8 to 19—about half of which were sports-related—and 8- to 13-year-olds accounted for about one-third of the visits, according to Dr. Lisa Bakhos and colleagues at Brown University, Injury Prevention Center and Rhode Island Hospital/Hasbro Children's Hospital in Providence, who analyzed information from two national databases for the study.

Although organized team sport participation declined from 1997 to 2007, emergency department visits

Youth Emergency Department Visits for Traumatic Brain Injuries Are Increasing

Estimated percent of sports-related emergency department visits that were for traumatic brain injuries for persons nineteen years old and younger in the United States.

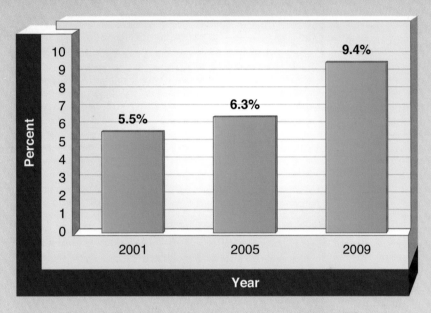

Taken from: US Centers for Disease Control and Prevention. "Nonfatal Traumatic Brain Injuries Related to Sports and Recreation Activites Among Persons Aged ≤ 19 Years—United States, 2001–2009." *Morbidity and Mortality Weekly Report*, October 7, 2011.

for concussions increased among both young children and teens, the study found.

The study and the guidelines will boost awareness of the seriousness of concussions, said Dr. Gillian Hotz, director of the concussion program in the department of neurosurgery at the University of Miami Miller School of Medicine.

"Most kids are OK [after a concussion]," Hotz said. But more information has evolved, and health care experts know to take concussions more seriously and to be

A young boy is tested for a concussion. Doctors say the only effective treatment for concussion is plenty of rest. Doing homework, watching television, and playing video games may worsen symptoms.
(© AP Images/ Herald and Review, Mark Roberts)

sure kids are symptom-free before returning to play, she added.

Hotz suspects the number of concussions found in the study are underestimates, pointing out that many children are not seen in the emergency department but may visit their pediatrician instead, and others may not get medical attention at all.

Many Childhood Sports Injuries Are Preventable

Mary Brophy Marcus

In the following viewpoint Mary Brophy Marcus says that many of the more than 3.5 million childhood sports injuries that occur annually in the United States are preventable. Marcus suggests that over-use injuries, in particular, are avoidable. Parents and coaches are advised not to ignore children who complain of pain and to make sure kids get enough sleep and rest, have time for non-sports-related "play," and are generally "fit and strong."

Marcus writes about health issues for *USA Today*, a national newspaper.

P ediatrician Gary Emmett likes to share a little mantra with kids and parents: "A good day is a day when you read for an hour and run for an hour."

Perfect advice for families whose kids are heading back to school and sports.

But "running" doesn't mean hitting sports fields with the gusto of an NFL running back, says Emmett, director of in-patient pediatrics at Thomas Jefferson University Hospital in Philadelphia. Other pediatric experts who treat children with sports injuries agree.

More than 3.5 million kids 14 and under are treated for sports injuries each year, according to the American College of Emergency Physicians [ACEP].

But many are preventable, says the American Orthopedic Society for Sports Medicine. Its STOP (Sports Trauma and Overuse Prevention) Sports Injuries campaign started in 2007.

Overuse Injuries

The most common injuries include concussions, stress fractures, knee problems and overuse injuries; they are especially prevalent in young athletes who play the same

Staying properly hydrated can help athletes prevent sports injuries.
(© Mark Clarke/Photo Researchers, Inc.)

sport year-round, says Michael O'Brien, a sports medicine physician at Children's Hospital Boston.

"We see athletes of all ages with overuse injuries," he says, but kids' injuries are different. "Kids are not small adults. They have a very different physiology. We don't see rotator cuff injuries, we see growth plate overuse from repetitive micro trauma," says O'Brien. This type of injury outpaces the bones' ability to recover and can cause growth problems.

"It's not uncommon for me to treat kids who play a sport in school and then the same sport at night and on weekends on leagues," says orthopedic surgeon Vonda Wright, who specializes in sports medicine at the University of Pittsburgh Schools of the Health Sciences.

> **FAST FACT**
>
> According to the Centers for Disease Control and Prevention, more than half of all sports injuries in children are preventable.

Common overuse injuries include stress fractures in the back, which can occur in gymnasts and dancers, and what O'Brien calls "little league shoulder and elbow" from too much ball throwing.

X-rays can help diagnose a problem, and extended rest is pivotal to healing, even if a dedicated student athlete is averse to taking time off, says O'Brien. He advises parents and coaches not to ignore chronic pain when they see a child suffering.

His rule: If symptoms interrupt the three S's sleep, stride (limping, for example) or study, they need to be checked out by a medical expert.

Concussions are also common in school athletes, especially in the fall, when soccer and football are in full swing, says O'Brien. Head injuries are common in lacrosse, typically a spring sport, as well, he says. Brain injury is the leading cause of sports-related death in children, according to ACEP.

Knee troubles are an issue with young female athletes, says Wright. "Girls really need to condition and get stronger to maintain their fitness level as they mature

Youth Who Participate in Sports Face Risk of Injury

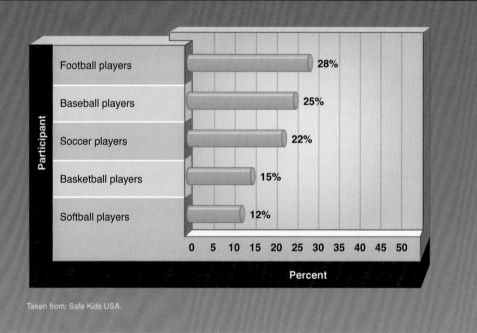

Percent of participants ages five to fourteen who were injured playing their respective sport

Participant	Percent
Football players	28%
Baseball players	25%
Soccer players	22%
Basketball players	15%
Softball players	12%

Taken from: Safe Kids USA.

into their pre-teen and teen years as athletes, she says. "We believe there's an epidemic of ACL (anterior cruciate ligament) injury in prepubescent girls who aren't conditioned. It's not only anatomy issues, that girls are built differently from boys and therefore more prone to knee injuries, but strength." says Wright, who performs risk assessments for girls sports teams.

Keep an eye out for undiagnosed asthma, too, says Neelay Gandhi, a family medicine physician at Baylor Family Medicine at Legacy in Plano, Texas.

"We see a lot of the time, kids start running or playing sports, and they say they can't breathe like everyone else. They may have exercise-induced asthma," says Gandhi.

He says sometimes the best way for doctors to diagnose it is to have children run around the doctor's office.

Keeping Kids Fit and Strong

Parents should also make sure kids get all of their vaccines and vision and hearing tests before playing sports, he says, as well as a good heart and lung exam.

Optimizing sleep time and recovery time and providing solid nutrition and fewer calorie-packed, sweetened sports drinks will help keep kids strong and fit, says O'Brien. Drinking water is a priority before, during and after exercise, he says.

Emmett says a daily multivitamin is a good idea, too, for "any kid who's exercising, even one who's not." And don't forget to let kids just play, he adds. For a healthy body and mind, "play—free play—is as important as competitive sports."

Soccer Players Should Wear Protective Headgear

Soccer Nation

In the following viewpoint Soccer Nation asserts that wearing headgear can help reduce concussions in female soccer players. Soccer Nation says that an NBC News television program that questioned the effectiveness of headgear in reducing soccer-related concussions in girls was incomplete. In the show it was suggested that evidence to support the use of headgear is lacking; however, the author claims that headgear's protective capacity was demonstrated by a Canadian study in 2007. According to Soccer Nation, headgear is not a silver bullet that can completely eliminate concussions, but the use of headgear along with proactive parents, coaches, and players can all contribute to fewer concussions.

Soccer Nation is an online news organization covering youth, college, and professional soccer teams in Southern California and the nation.

SOURCE: "NBC Report on Concussions—What Was Missed?" Soccer Nation, June 8, 2012. Copyright © 2012 by Soccer Nation. All rights reserved. Reproduced by permission.

On Thursday, June 7, [2012,] NBC's *Rock Center with Brian Williams* aired an episode on concussions in girls' soccer and the use of headgear as protection. In particular, the report by Kate Snow focused on the use of a padded headband produced by Full90 Sports and used by a former player featured in the episode, Natasha Helmick. While the show did bring up many important points, especially on the danger of concussions in girl soccer players, it also left out much.

In the report, Helmick recalled how she began using the headgear after suffering from a concussion, with the idea that it would prolong her playing career. She also admitted that she played more aggressively on the field with the headgear, believing that it would protect her from further concussions. However, she did suffer additional concussions and eventually had to give up the sport she loved.

The report seemed to focus mostly on the failure of the headgear to prevent additional concussions for this particular player, but did not discuss its possible effectiveness for others. It also minimized the importance of parents, coaches and players being proactive about reducing the occurrence of head trauma that can lead to concussions. The impression left from the interview with Helmick's parents was that they saw the headgear as the sole solution to concussions, rather than one piece of the answer.

One concern Snow brought up was that there was no convincing study that indicated headgear could protect players from concussions in soccer. However, a peer-reviewed study done by researchers at the Mc-Gill University Health Center in Canada ("The Effect of Protective Headgear on Head Injuries and Concussions in Adolescent Football [Soccer] Players") shows that players not wearing headgear were 2.65 times more likely to suffer a concussion than those wearing protective equipment. The study, which was published in the *British Journal of Sport Medicine* in 2007, also found that girls are far more likely than boys to suffer concussions while playing soccer.

According to the study, "While being female increased the risk of experiencing a concussion, the use of football [soccer] headgear decreased this risk during the 2006 football season." It also stated specifically that "football headgear provided protection against concussions in the population studied."

Jeff Skeen, founder and CEO of Full90 Sports, pointed out that no product can give total protection from concussions, but that other options that have been discussed have their own problems. "Banning heading is a non-starter," he said, "and better training and neck strengthening doesn't work for the best athletes in the world. Henri Thierry [Major League Soccer player for the New York Red Bulls] has gotten a few concussions, so it is not lack of training."

Skeen explained that there is a fine line between providing protection for a player's head and violating FIFA [International Federation of Association Football] restrictions in Equipment Law 4. "If I wore an American football helmet that helmet would be more successful in reducing the likelihood of concussions than our Full90 headband, but it would violate FIFA LAW 4 and change the game."

In the report it was implied that Skeen and Full90 Sports are more interested in selling a product than in actually protecting players—a charge that Skeen vehemently denies.

"I'm not doing this for the money," he said. "I've suffered multiple concussions myself, one of which required brain surgery for a subdural hematoma. And after watching my own daughter suffer from post-concussion syndrome for years after she received concussions while playing soccer, I chose to dedicate my time to finding ways to reduce soccer-

FAST FACT

According to data from Ohio State University, high school female soccer players suffer concussions at a rate of 3.83 per 10,000 athletes.

related head injuries. I have personally invested a significant amount of money in Full90, worked diligently for over 10 years, and have not been paid. Furthermore, if I ever make any profit, I will donate it to head injury research."

At some point parents, coaches and players have to take the initiative when it comes to reducing the incidence and long-term effects of head injuries. Better training on identifying possible concussions and more focus on making sure players are ready to return to the field both will help in this area. Also needed is more study on the causes of concussions in youth players and the role of some type of headgear as protection.

"While the NBC segment did not show all the points we touched upon during the full interview, we can still declare a victory," Skeen said. "When we began this journey over 10 years ago, the soccer community was denying

An English soccer goalie wears the latest in protective headgear for soccer players. Proponents of such gear say that along with action by parents, coaches, and players, wearing protective gear will reduce concussions. (© AP Images/Scott Heppel)

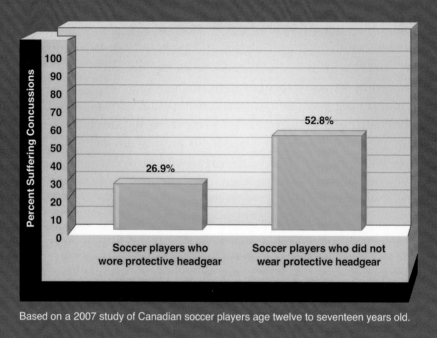

Headgear–Wearing Soccer Players Suffer Fewer Concussions

Percent Suffering Concussions

- 26.9% — Soccer players who wore protective headgear
- 52.8% — Soccer players who did not wear protective headgear

Based on a 2007 study of Canadian soccer players age twelve to seventeen years old.

Taken from: J. Scott Delaney, et al. "The Effect of Protective Headgear on Head Injuries and Concussions in Adolescent Football (Soccer) Players," *British Journal of Sports Medicine*, 2007.

concussions were a problem and that soccer was a contact sport. Today, the discussion is on reducing head injuries, which was our goal." . . .

Head injuries are a reality in soccer, as they are in any sport. Football is rife with stories of players who have suffered multiple concussions, baseball routinely sees the results of the impact of the ball against heads, and even basketball players face possible injury from flying elbows as they jostle for the ball. There is no way to prevent every injury from occurring, nor should there be. What is important is making sure that players are properly trained and equipped for their sport and that, should a head injury happen, they are treated and observed by qualified specialists before they return to the field.

The National Football League Is Largely Responsible for Players' Concussions

Jerome Solomon

In the following viewpoint Jerome Solomon asserts that the National Football League (NFL) is complicit in football players' concussions. According to Solomon, those who say the players are solely responsible for their concussions are wrong. He says that former players had no idea of the risk of concussions they faced when they started playing the game. The NFL is responsible, says Solomon. There is a link between concussions and playing football, and the league has failed to protect players by refusing to acknowledge this.

Solomon is a sports columnist with the *Houston Chronicle*, a Texas daily newspaper.

I keep hearing from people who say former NFL players knew what they were getting into when they started playing football, so significant brain injuries are just part of the game and they should get over it.

Seriously?

SOURCE: Jerome Solomon, "Those Who Put Concussion Onus on the Players Aren't Thinking Clearly," *Houston Chronicle*, May 14, 2012. Copyright © 2012 by the Houston Chronicle. All rights reserved. Reproduced by permission.

Green Bay Packers quarterback Aaron Rodgers sits stunned after suffering a blow to the head that resulted in a concussion. Critics believe that the National Football League is responsible for the concussions pro players sustain during practice and games. (© **Mark Cunningham/Detroit Lions/Getty Images**)

Even as one who thinks there are too many lawsuits over some perceived mistreatment, I believe that is a ridiculous, almost indefensible position to take in this discussion. People who so casually say such things are ignorant.

The recent talk about concussions has felt like overkill, and overkill can make you think things that just aren't true. If you spend enough time on Facebook or Twitter (or listening to clowns on talk radio), you'd think Kate Upton is the most beautiful woman EVER and a 10-second dance she did is the hottest thing EVER. Wrong and wrong.

Similarly, talk about concussions (and jealousy over the money athletes make) has some people thinking anyone who ever played professional football had to know about concussion issues before he started playing, so he deserves little sympathy for health issues he might have at the age of 40.

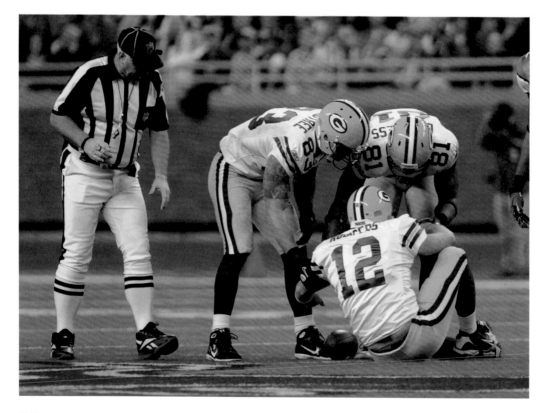

I'm not saying it is all on the NFL, but to put it all on the players makes little sense.

First, consider that when NFL players began playing football, when they were 7, 8 or 9 years old, nobody asked them if they were willing to suffer brain damage that might lead to significant health problems after their careers were over.

If your child's pee wee football league holds such a discussion before letting children play, please get in touch with me, I'd like to attend one of those meetings.

Will that stop boys from wanting to play football? I doubt it, but I bet more parents won't let them.

Secondly, people who think players knew what they were getting into act as if we have been having these brain-injury discussions for 50 years. We really haven't.

People know what boxing can do to the brain. The NFL has always maintained that helmets kept that from happening in football. End of discussion.

The first case of chronic traumatic encephalopathy (CTE) in a professional football player wasn't detected in a retired football player until 2002. That was only 10 years ago, in 50-year-old Steelers Hall of Fame center Mike Webster, who suffered from dementia and depression.

Dr. Bennet I. Omalu, who studied Webster's brain and many others, believes there is a direct link between repeated blows to the head and permanent brain damage. Makes sense, doesn't it? Well, he had trouble getting the NFL to agree.

Dr. Ira Casson used to be the co-chairman of the NFL Mild Traumatic Brain Injury Committee (don't you love how the league put mild in front of traumatic?), which was formed in 1994. Each time an independent study

> **FAST FACT**
>
> According to a study published in the journal *Neurology* in 2012, retired pro football players are four times more likely to suffer from Alzheimer's disease and amyotrophic lateral sclerosis (ALS) than is the general US population.

Former NFL Players Suffered Concussions but Most Say It Was Worth It

92%
Suffered at least one concussion

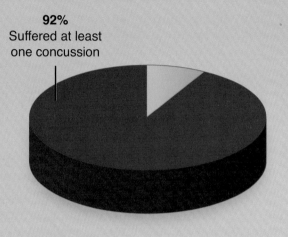

Question: "Knowing what you know now (about concussions), would you do your NFL career over again?"

77%
Yes

23%
No

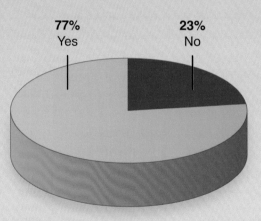

Taken from: "Sporting News Concussion Report: NFL Career Worth It? Two Hall of Famers Say No." *Sporting News*, August 16, 2012.

such as Omalu's was introduced, Casson slammed it as being inconclusive.

I'm not saying Casson is wrong, but he is out on a limb darn near by himself. You don't think the NFL wanted him to lean a particular direction in his findings?

In a way, the NFL has been telling us over and over that players have nothing to worry about.

The league didn't even start studying retired players until 2007. And then all it did was a phone survey with 120 former players. Even in that small sample, the league found that those players suffered from dementia and other memory issues at a rate significantly higher than the non-football playing population.

What was Casson's (thus the league's) stance?

"What I take from this report is there's a need for further studies to see whether or not this finding is going to pan out," he said.

This, while several studies involving brain tissue analysis were already showing evidence of brain damage in former football players.

Just two years ago [in 2010], Casson, who didn't resign from the NFL post until the end of 2009, testified before Congress that he still wasn't convinced football causes brain damage.

"My position is that there is not enough valid, reliable or objective scientific evidence at present to determine whether or not repeat head impacts in professional football result in long-term brain damage," he said.

Again, as crazy as it sounds, Casson could be right in saying that we still don't know what we know.

So we're still waiting for the NFL to say concussions can cause long-term problems.

Does that mean the league should be sued by every guy who ever put on a uniform? Hardly. But to say players knew what they were getting into is simply not true.

So please, stop.

The National Football League Should Not Be Held Responsible for Players' Concussions

Ryan Gorman

In the following viewpoint Ryan Gorman contends that the National Football League (NFL) is not to blame for concussions, players are. Gorman says the 2012 suicide of iconic NFL player Junior Seau is tragic, but it should not be used as a reason to blame the NFL. Gorman says that football is a violent sport, injuries have always been a part of the game, and there is nothing the NFL can do about it. Instead, he says, players, with their cavalier attitudes toward injuring opposition players, have no one but themselves to blame.
  Gorman is a sportswriter for the news website Policymic.

Junior Seau's death at 43, from an apparent suicide, has provided a household name for those who claim the NFL [National Football League] needs to change. Their argument is that the league is to blame for the players who suffer so many brain injuries. The problem with their argument is that it's not the league's fault, it's the players who do it to themselves.

Football Has Always Been Violent

Football is a violent sport. Players are constantly hurt and there are TV timeouts for injuries multiple times per game. Every type of injury, from a jammed finger, to paralysis, and everything in between, has happened on the football field at all levels of competitive organized play. Yet people only want to point the finger at the NFL.

For the sake of argument, let's whittle our focus down to concussions. In 2011, there were 171 concussions/head injuries in the NFL, according to the website *Concussion Blog*. That is 12 more than the previous season, despite numerous efforts from the NFL to lessen the severity of head injuries to its players.

Only two teams, the Cincinnati Bengals and Houston Texans, had no incidence of concussion all season; though the Texans starting and backup quarterbacks did miss the majority of the season due to a fractured right foot and an injured collarbone, respectively.

The NCAA [National Collegiate Athletic Association], for the sake of comparison, reported 177 concussions during the 2011 college football season according to the *Concussion Blog*. Since the NCAA has far more teams than the 32-team NFL does, that actually works out to a lower rate of concussions than in the pro games.

Concussions go far back into the lore of the NFL. When the great Frank Gifford retired in 1960, after Chuck Bednarik's vicious tackle gave him a concussion; he was only 30. Gifford eventually came back 18 months later, but was never the same and didn't even play the same position. The hit was clean, shoulder first, and still almost paralyzed him. Gifford told the *New York Times* that he found out a vertebra in his neck had fractured and healed on its own. He didn't find out until he was told by a doctor over 40 years later.

In 1995, former New York Jets slot receiver Al Toon told the *LA Times* he had "more than five and probably less than 20" concussions in his eight year NFL career. He couldn't remember all of them. Suicide crossed his mind, not the act itself he says, but "life was very frustrating." His son Nick was just drafted by the New Orleans Saints to play wide receiver.

Former 49ers quarterback Steve Young had seven diagnosed concussions in his career, (four in his last three seasons,) before he retired in 2000 after being knocked out of his last game with—you guessed it—a concussion. Former Dallas Cowboys quarterback Troy Aikman sustained 10 concussions in his career, four in his last two seasons, before retiring in 2001 after only 12 seasons.

Junior Seau was never diagnosed with a concussion, but was said to have told those close to him that he experienced "multiple head injuries" in his career, says *ESPN*. Seau being a football player and dying of suicide, made people immediately jump on the suicide-by-concussion bandwagon.

Why all this talk about players that aren't Seau when talking about his suicide? The answer is simple. No matter what rules, fines, or suspensions the league makes, there will be head injuries and concussions. Players like James Harrison of the Steelers care more about injuring players than playing the game cleanly.

Point the Finger at Players

Harrison's cavalier attitude about how he routinely injures other players is what is wrong with football. The macho culture of the league is to hurt others—Saints bounty program anyone?[1]—and then lie about one's own injuries to avoid losing your spot in the rotation, since contracts are usually not guaranteed.

> **FAST FACT**
>
> As of August 2012, according to the Associated Press, 3,377 players had sued the NFL, charging that not enough was done to inform them of the dangers of concussions in the past, or to take care of them in the present.

---

1. In 2012 the New Orleans Saints football franchise was sanctioned by the NFL for awarding "bounties"—rewards—to its players who succeeded in injuring an opposing player.

Seau never told anyone about his head injuries or that he needed help. Had he, the network of support and care he would have received would have rivaled any in the world.

Concussions have long been a part of the NFL. There isn't much that can be done about them unless the game is abolished altogether. Since we all know that isn't going

Former pro football great Junior Seau's suicide in 2012 and the condition of his mental health due to concussions sustained in his career sparked criticism of the NFL's role in preventing and treating concussions. (© Larry Maurer/Getty Images)

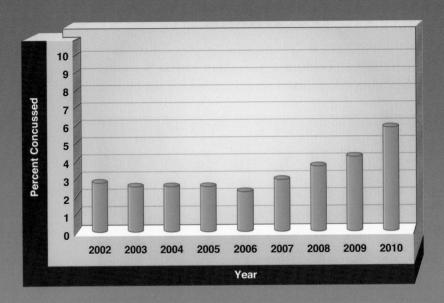

Percentage of NFL Players Suffering at Least One Concussion

Taken from: Total Outsiders. Edgeworth Economics. "Dangers of the Game NFLPA Injury Report," January 26, 2011. Linked to Tim Wendel. "The NFL Lockouts Healthcare Data Revealed." *Esquire*, January 27, 2011.

to happen, the next best thing to do would be to teach children playing the game the right way to tackle from pee-wee football, all the way through to high school, and college, so they aren't head hunting in the NFL.

Instead of pointing fingers at the league, point them at the players. They are the ones who hurt each other, who lie about their health and injuries, and who laugh at fines larger than what most of us make in a year. Junior Seau's death is an absolute tragedy, but no one made him mislead trainers and medical staff about the head injuries he sustained during his career.

CHAPTER **3**

Personal Experiences with Sports Injuries

A Mother Responds When Her Son Suffers a Sports-Related Brain Injury

Victoria Tilney McDonough

In the following viewpoint Victoria Tilney McDonough tells the story of Jean Rickerson, whose son's concussion opened her eyes to the risks of brain injuries for young athletes. After suffering a hit to the head during a high school football game in 2008, Rickerson's son, Drew, began acting strangely. Although his coaches, doctors, and even other family members did not think Drew was seriously injured, Jean knew something was wrong. She began researching sports-related head injuries and learned about conditions such as traumatic brain injury (TBI) and chronic traumatic encephalopathy (CTE). Finding a lack of awareness on the issue, Rickerson created the website, SportsConcussions.org as a resource to help educate coaches, parents, and athletes about the dangers of concussions in youth sports.

McDonough is a writer for BrainLine.org, a website of the public radio station WETA in Washington, D.C.

Photo on previous page. The rehabilitation of a sports injury can be a long and arduous process. (© Sarah L. Voisin/The Washington Post/Getty Images)

SOURCE: Victoria Tilney McDonough, "A Mother's Intuition," Brainline.org, a WETA website, 2012. Copyright © 2012 by Brainline.org. All rights reserved. Reproduced by permission.

Around 6 PM on Friday nights in Sequim, Washington, the collective adrenaline starts to pump. Cars around the high school stadium are parked at all angles, a herky-jerky pattern of mosaics. Hoodies are zipped against the fall air, sodas snap open, coffee and cocoa steam from thermos cups. Families find their favorite spots on the bleachers, friends hug, teenagers whisper and shriek with new gossip. Then, the pulse quickens as the players storm the field. The stadium lights beam yellow and promising above the night.

Friday Night Lights

Sequim is a football town. If you play, you're a hero. If you are the parent or teacher or friend of a player, you have clout. Some towns are just like that. Jean Rickerson is a Sequim football mother. Her son, Drew, is a highly acclaimed high school quarterback. But the nature of her role as a football mother changed one night in 2008 when Drew, then 16, took an intense helmet-to-helmet hit.

"I videotaped all of Drew's games, but that night was too foggy," says Jean. And because of the fog, she didn't see the hit clearly. After the collision, Drew played for another 15 minutes. He threw a touchdown pass and then scored a touchdown. As his teammates ran crazy with excitement, he tossed the ball to the ref and staggered to the bench. "There was something odd about the way he ran off the field. I suddenly had a sinking feeling," says Jean.

Drew sat on the bench for the remaining 45 minutes of the game. Jean watched her son through the fog and the rows of bobbing heads, but his back was to her and she couldn't see his face. He kept dropping his helmet, leaning sideways. He seemed to have no interest in the game—his game, his team. "I will never forgive myself for watching him, knowing in my gut that something was not right, and not doing anything about it," she says.

When the game was over, Drew stood up and turned. Jean saw his face and knew immediately that something was dreadfully wrong. His eyes looked empty. During those 45 minutes, he had not been able to tell anyone he was hurt because he couldn't speak, and he had started to lose his vision and his hearing. He hadn't lost consciousness, but everything was blurry and confusing, jiggling sounds and blob-like shapes behind diaphanous glass.

Jean ran to get the rescue squad who checked him out. Despite his unevenly dilated pupils and his inability to speak, the EMTs [emergency medical technicians] said they didn't think he needed any help much less transport to the ER [emergency room]. His coaches waved and told him they'd see him for practice at 8 a.m. the next morning. Jean became angry. "What would you do if your son were in this condition?" she asked the EMTs. She insisted they take Drew to the ER. So, two-and-a-half hours after the collision on the field, he was at the hospital, a delay that would have been disastrous for some seriously concussed players.

After an evaluation and CT [computed tomography] scan, Drew was cleared to go home. The doctors said he'd be good as new. He'd be back at school Monday. He'd be out there on the field leading the Sequim Wolves. "We believed the doctors," said Jean. "We didn't know enough not to; we didn't know anything."

Cleared to Play—Again

For the Rickersons, especially Drew, the weekend passed like a [Federico] Fellini film [known for their surrealism]. Nothing felt real. Nothing felt normal, predictable. Drew would stand up, see stars, and fall back down onto the sofa or his bed. He slept constantly. Jean thought a short walk and some fresh air would help her son feel better. But he could barely make it a block or two. TV and video games revealed the fact that Drew had little-to-no short-term memory and no analytical thinking skills. "Things were obviously not right with Drew, but what did I know?" says Jean. "I was terrified all weekend but held those feelings in check because the doctors were not concerned. I had no idea how serious all of this was."

By Monday, Jean was panicked. During an office visit, their family doctor told her not to be concerned. Again, Drew was cleared to play and return to school. She left the appointment and found another doctor, seeking someone more educated. They couldn't get in to see that next doctor for another two days. After that second appointment—now five days later—Drew couldn't move his limbs. He was rushed to a trauma center two hours away in Seattle where CT and MRI [magnetic resonance imaging] scans both came back negative. We were not given any instructions as to what to avoid, or any other after-care advice. We were on our own, again."

Jean cried all the way home. "For the first time, I realized I had absolutely no idea what to do to help my son," she says. "I felt I had exhausted possibilities on the [Olympic] peninsula for care, and if the trauma center in Seattle didn't offer hope, I was lost. I was my son's only hope and I was completely uneducated. It was a desperate time."

In town, at school, on the football field, and even with the rest of the Rickerson family, Drew was expected back. He was the star quarterback, after all. He was Drew. Jean wondered if she was being hysterical. Was she being reactive, over-protective? She doubted herself, but in the end, her gut prevailed and Drew did not play. She could live with being the hated mother in a town where football is revered above almost all else.

Bleak Times

The next ten weeks were bleak. Drew stayed home from school for two weeks then returned part-time. He would attend classes from 8–10 a.m. only to return home exhausted with no recollection of what he had learned. "These were very scary weeks," says Jean. "I didn't know if this was going to be permanent. Would Drew be able to go to college? Play sports again? Have a job? Function in the world?"

As the weeks passed, although Drew was starting to feel better and act more like his old self, Jean knew he was still not totally back. "I'm his mother. I just knew," she says. Burning the midnight oil on the Internet, she knew there had to be someone, somewhere who could help her son. Finally, Jean found a doctor connected with the University of Washington—120 miles from Sequim—who listened and who didn't simply send them on their way. He recommended that Drew undergo a full neuropsychological evaluation—a full battery of tests that looks at the person's language as well as his cognitive, motor, behavioral, and executive functioning. Drew scored in the 16th percentile on certain portions of the tests; he obviously had a lot more healing to do.

During those ten weeks as Drew struggled to relearn basic math and recognize words that had come easily in third grade, Jean started to research sports concussions. A retired video producer, she was on a mission to learn all she could and then spread the word about concussion awareness to players, parents, coaches, and anyone else involved in youth sports. . . .

"Just a Mother"

Jean didn't want any other parents to have to go through what she did. "It was frightening not knowing what was wrong, not being able to help my own child," she says. "Once you know, you can take action. That is empowering."

She started going to clinics, hospitals, and schools. Armed with fact sheets and articles from the Centers for Disease Control and Prevention, she would try to raise awareness about the dangers of concussions in youth sports. Some people were open to sharing the information. Others, less so. One local clinic threw her out—twice. "They didn't think mild TBI [traumatic brain injury] was an issue; they said TBI symptoms are psychological. I was just a mother, they implied, they were the experts," she says. . . .

The untimely death of actress Natasha Richardson from a fall on the ski slopes and the passing of the Lystedt Law—one of the nation's toughest return-to-play law aiding young athletes concussion recovery, passed in Washington State in May 2009—certainly helped reinforce Jean's message. In June 2009, Jean held a conference at a local high school. More than 200 people attended, including school superintendents, first responders, pediatricians, young athletes, coaches, and parents.

In January 2010, Jean launched her website, www.sportsconcussions.org. She picked a website for the hub of her campaign since she was able to eventually track down care for her son via the web and she also learned that the Internet is where most parents go first for information. She wants parents, coaches, and players to have sound information if they ever need it. "There is an important conversation out there about concussions and we, as parents, coaches, and players, need to be a part of it," she says.

FAST FACT

According to the Centers for Disease Control and Prevention, as many as three hundred thousand sports and recreation-related concussions occur each year in the United States.

Dinner Tables to State Houses

The Lystedt Law—named for Zackery Lystedt who at 13 sustained a life-changing brain injury while playing football—requires medical clearance of youth athletes under the age of 18 suspected of sustaining a concussion before they can be sent back into a game, practice, or training. And since its 2009 adoption, other states have followed suit.

"The passage of these state laws has been tremendous," says Jean. "We've already seen changes being made in our communities and unprecedented conversations have been taking place from dinner tables to state houses." And the fact that the dangers of traumatic

Zackery Lystedt (pictured) suffered a concussion in a football game. Washington state's Lystedt Law, which requires athletes under the age of eighteen who are suspected of having sustained a concussion to be cleared by a physician before they can play, practice, or train, was named after him. (© AP Images/ Elaine Thompson)

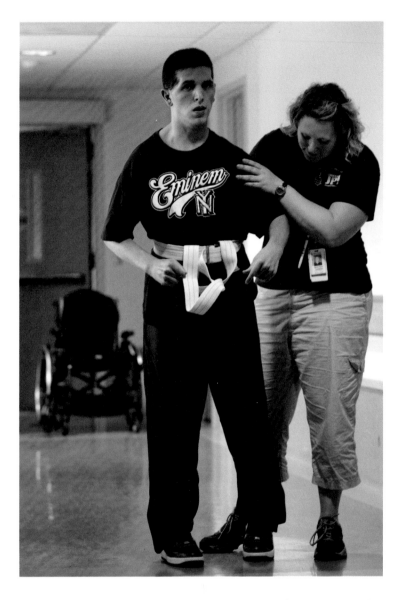

brain injury and cumulative concussion has been in the media—from the NFL [National Football League] to the military—has certainly helped raise awareness.

But there is still a long way to go. For example, the helmet that Drew wore playing in the game in which he was hit had un-inflated padding in it. The inside was hard as a rock. Why was the padding not inflated? If it had been, it would not have fit. As in other athletic departments in countless school districts across the country, helmets are "refurbished" and checked only one time a year. Athletic equipment safety standards vary district to district and have been lax. A 2011 study conducted through the Virginia Tech National Impact Database, showed that even some NFL helmets did not meet standards.

Slow but Positive Change

But Jean is optimistic—and she has no intention of ceasing her mission to spread awareness about TBI in sports. In addition to running her website, she speaks at conferences or collaborates in meetings like the recent NFL Summit in DC, which focused on the NFL's mission to promote passage of the Lystedt Law in all 50 states. She also oversees ten state representatives in seven states—volunteers who attend conferences, share materials, and raise awareness.

Her work is paying off. Jean is seeing change in her own community as well as in the media. Her school district recently mandated that all equipment, like football helmets, be checked before every game, instead of every season. And helmets older than ten years have to be retired. She also sees more coaches and parents keeping kids from play until they have been cleared by their own doctors—an enormous accomplishment in a town where football and winning reign supreme. . . .

She hears more conversations, too. Parents of youth athletes, like her, are very concerned about what's happening in the NFL and how repeat blows to the head might affect their children's present and future. What about kids that start tackle football at 10? How many hits to the head will accumulate during hundreds of practices and games? Will they be candidates for chronic traumatic encephalopathy [CTE] or early onset dementia? The scientific jury is still out.

"To Thine Own Self Be True"

One hundred and twenty days after his helmet-to-helmet collision, Drew was cleared to play baseball. But it wasn't until a full year later that Drew returned to his pre-injury levels of reading and cognitive thinking. He was a lucky kid. Some athletes who sustain a serious hit never return fully to their previous selves—physically, emotionally, and intellectually.

Drew did play football again in 2010–2011. "It was a hard choice, and a scary choice," says Jean. "He is at higher risk now if he gets hit; he will be at higher risk for the rest of his life. But he is a football star and where we live, football is everything. If I had said no, I honestly don't think our family would still be intact."

In fall 2011, Drew started his freshman year at Pacific Lutheran University in Tacoma [Washington]. He plays baseball, not football. It was entirely his choice. Sometimes kids do listen to their mothers.

A Doctor Discusses Brain Injuries in Boxers and Mixed Martial Arts Fighters

Charles Bernick, as told to Jack Encarnacao

Charles Bernick is a neurologist and associate medical director of the Cleveland Clinic Lou Ruvo Center for Brain Health in Las Vegas, Nevada. In the following viewpoint he is interviewed by Jack Encarnacao of *Sherdog Rewind,* an Internet radio program of Sherdog.com, a mixed martial arts (MMA) website. Encarnacao asks Bernick to describe a study that he is conducting of some two hundred boxers and MMA fighters. The goals of the study, called the Professional Fighters Brain Health Study, include determining the earliest changes of damage that occur in the brains of fighters who suffer hits to the head and identifying those fighters who are the most susceptible to suffering long-term brain changes as a result of repeated head trauma. Bernick tells Encarnacao that he hopes the study will provide information to allow fighters and regulatory agencies to make informed decisions about continued participation in the sport.

Sherdog.com: Tell us where the study is at and what exactly it seeks to determine.

[Charles] Bernick: This is officially titled the "Professional Fighters Brain Health Study," so this is looking, as a group, at both mixed martial arts athletes and boxers, and there are several aims of this study. One is to be able to determine or identify the earliest changes of damage in the brain by using some of the newer techniques we have available with MRI [magnetic resonance imaging] scans, as well as other potential markers of injury. This could be chemicals in the blood or even changes in speech patterns and so on. The second is really to be able to determine which individual may be on their way to developing these long-term complications of repetitive head trauma. The most common one we hear about is Chronic Traumatic Encephalopathy, which of course has been in the news with the tragedy of [former National Football League (NFL) star and suicide] Junior Seau. And then the third is to find out why some people develop this chronic brain condition and others don't, even with the same exposure, and whether that's due to genetics or environmental factors or whatever. So those are the three overarching aims of the project. We started this about a year ago. We have now about 180-plus fighters that have participated in this study, and what the study involves is looking at these participants once a year for at least four years. We'd like to keep it going longer, but if we can get four years of information out of a substantial number of individuals, we'll have learned a tremendous amount about a subject that we know very little about. We feel that the damage and the changes in these conditions start when people are actively fighting, and that's where we have to look first if we're going to detect these earliest changes.

How do you recruit fighters into participating?

We in some sense have a carrot. In Nevada and many states, there is a requirement to have an MRI scan as part of licensure. So because in this study individuals get an

MRI scan once a year, they get this potential $1,000 test for free. So we know that a lot of the fighters come in basically to save money, and we also offer some of the blood tests that they require for licensure: the HIV, Hepatitis B, Hepatitis C. That brings in some fighters. But the hope is that once they understand the importance of it and the value to their own lives, they'll stick with it. We receive a variety of responses. Some people come in, again, just for the free tests. But some people do care, and they want to know, particularly if they're later in their career. We have tremendous support from our Nevada Athletic Commission, which has really been helpful to us, and, of course, the UFC [Ultimate Fighting Championship] has been a tremendous supporter. So we have the backing of the industry in some sense, and, unlike other sports, they've been with us right from the start and they've supported this type of research. When we see athletes here, I think they all know, or most of them understand there is a risk of being in a sport where you may sustain repetitive concussions or sub-concussive injuries. For many of them, it's a livelihood. They've been in this sport a long time. It's a challenge. They love it. And I think what we're trying to do is not discourage people from participating [in boxing and MMA] but somehow make it safer, make the sport safer.

Could this be a situation where you'll be able to put solid science in front of a fighter that proves he has reached the point of no return and is risking serious mental health complications if he continues to fight?

I think it will go two ways. I think the hope is, yeah, having objective information that we can present to the athletes so they can decide. So that's, of course, the most important part. And, by the way, it doesn't have to be all or none. We might find that there's a certain frequency of fighting or density of fighting that becomes too dangerous at a certain point. So it may be that instead of saying, "You can't fight at all" or "You should stop completely," it may be that, well, you're limited to fighting only twice a year and then training a certain amount before those fights. So we'll have to see how this pans out. But, of course, aside from the individual fighter, as you might imagine, regulatory agencies would like this information, too, because these athletic commissions are having to make decisions, in some sense, arbitrarily on whether a fighter can continue their career, because they don't have any objective markers to help them. And I think it's fair to everybody in the sport if there were actually objective measures that can tell someone whether they should continue on or not, or, as I say, can fight a lesser amount. Or perhaps at some point we'll have treatments, treatments that you can actually institute even before significant damage occurs.

When it comes to commissions making judgments about a fighter's brain health, what makes it arbitrary? What don't commissions have access to in making these decisions?

I think at this point . . . we have no objective findings. That's the problem, I think, at the moment. I mean, unless somebody has an obvious structural problem in the brain that we know threatens their health. Short of that, there is no objective measures for commissions to make decisions. So what do they do? They look, at least with boxers, (at) how they've been doing the last few fights. Are they starting to really lose their abilities? Are they getting knocked out earlier? And so on. So a lot of it is just kind of, again, intuitive, based on not tremendously objective measures, and we don't have objective measures now. But the hope from a project such as ours and maybe others like it is that we'll be able to say, "Alright, if you have such and such a change on your MRI scan between your last year and this year, then some disease is starting. You're in trouble, and you better stop."

FAST FACT

According to a study conducted by researchers at the Center for Injury Research and Policy, the number of boxing injuries treated in emergency rooms in the United States increased by 211 percent from 1990 (5,361 injuries) to 2008 (nearly 17,000 injuries).

Give us an idea of the type of change in a fighter's brain that might be a sign of trouble.

There's a number of changes that we can actually measure on just a garden-variety MRI scan. One is we can measure the volume or size of certain areas of the brain, and, of course, if there is damage to that area, it will shrink in size. So we can measure that shrinkage, and, again, if the rate of shrinkage exceeds what you really would expect, that might be a dangerous sign. Or another common technique that's readily available is looking at the fibers that course across the brain. We can actually visualize those and we can see what percentage of them are damaged. For example, maybe if there's an increase in the percentage that's damaged, that may be a sign. Or we're now able to measure the connections between different areas of the brain and [if those get] disrupted a certain amount, then that might be a sign. So it is looking like there may be distinct markers on imaging of the brain that can give us, really, information on if a disease is starting, if Chronic Traumatic Encephalopathy is starting. A new technique that's not available, but it's being developed, is actually to be able to image tau (a protein in the brain that is connected to Alzheimer's and dementia). This would be crucial. I mean, if we could actually measure it in individuals through scanning the brain, we would in some sense be able to identify the disease at its earliest stage. These things are not that far off, and, hopefully, within the next five years, 10 years, we'll have these very objective markers.

Explain, if you could, the tau protein.

Tau protein is a normal protein. What it really is involved in normally is the scaffolding or the skeleton of the brain cell, so it keeps the form of it intact. It turns out when tau changes its form that scaffolding just collapses, and then the cell gets damaged and machinery gets damaged. So we think tau is a marker of damage to the cell, and it's really interesting; it's now been shown that tau can move from one cell to another. Because one of the perplexities is, well, if you stop fighting, why should a disease progress? And it may progress because once you have that tau there, it actually can spread from cell to cell over time. So it's really kind of on the forefront of science now—is understanding how trauma leads to this tau being deposited and, again, what we can do to maybe prevent it from spreading. It could be a vaccine. It could be medications. We don't know yet. But there may be ways to prevent that.

So is tau what causes brain degeneration or is it just a marker that degeneration is happening?

Well, again, we don't know, that's a very good question. We don't know that. What we would need to do is understand it probably first in animal models, and there are animal models of repetitive head trauma, and we may get some idea from that. But the smoking gun is that (tau) seems to be fundamental, or the characteristic finding, in Chronic Traumatic Encephalopathy [CTE]. And there's other findings as well. But somehow tau plays an important role. . . .

Why has CTE suddenly become so knowable?

I think it's just the attention. First of all, you have to look for it. In other words, unless you stain the brain in a certain way to look for tau and do more sophisticated neuro-pathological studies, you're not going to find it. And, so, I think it was the attention that's come from the NFL and such. Now we've studied more brains, and there just seems to be an abnormal amount of people—athletes—with CTE. And it's probably there all the time; it's just that nobody looked or we didn't have the staining techniques to look. There was this recent article of a study from Boston University about the veterans coming back from Iraq who have blast injuries, passed away and at autopsy had changes of CTE from that exposure. It's becoming clear that head trauma, and particularly repetitive head trauma, certainly raises your risk of developing this complication. And I think now we're seeing it just across the board in different areas of society. . . .

The logical conclusion of the type of study you're doing is that eventually you'll be able to cull data that can end a fighter's career. I imagine at some point there would be some friction with promoters if that prevents him and the fighter from making money.

Well, yeah, that's going to be up to the regulatory agencies. It definitely will affect the fighter and the promoter. But, really, for the benefit of the sport, you really probably don't want tomato cans [fighters with low skills or who are past their prime and thus easy to defeat] around, people that are just losing their skill. That doesn't serve anybody. So I think, you know, it really benefits the sport itself to try to actually have people that are losing

Charles Bernick's study of professional fighters attempted to determine changes in the brains of fighters who have suffered repeated blows to the head and to identify those fighters most at risk for long-term brain damage. (© **AP Images/ The Canadian Press,** **Darryl Dyck)**

their skill because changes are happening in the brain to probably get out before they get more damage and lose their skills.

It might be self-evident, but tell us what's at stake here. What is on the line for these fighters in terms of why this study is so important?

I guess when you're young, you don't think about these things. But, of course, we see people further down the line, when you're late 40s, 50s—which is actually not very old—or 60s, where you have families that become part of the equation that suffer from this. So not only do you in some sense lose the athlete themselves and their quality of life, but it affects families around them. Although people in combat sports make up a very small portion of society, in general, it's an important component, in that it reflects not only fighting but other sports that involve contact, military, people who are injured with head trauma. All these different parts of society can end up the same way. And I think if we understand it in the sport of MMA or boxing, we can translate these types of things and really help people throughout society.

GLOSSARY

Achilles tendon   A band of connective tissue that connects calf muscles to the heel bone.

acute   In medical terminology, a rapidly developing condition; it comes on quickly and often causes severe symptoms but lasts only a short time.

anterior cruciate ligament (ACL)   One of the four major ligaments that provide stability to the human knee. The ACL is on the front (anterior) of the knee joint in humans.

arthroscopy   A minimally invasive surgical procedure for diagnosing and treating joint problems.

cartilage   Tough but flexible tissue that covers the ends of bones at joints. It also gives shape and support to other parts of the body.

chronic injury   An injury that happens over a period of time and is usually the result of repetitive training, such as running, overhand throwing, or serving in tennis.

chronic traumatic encephalopathy (CTE)   A progressive degenerative brain disease, usually diagnosed postmortem in professional wrestlers, football players, hockey players, and other individuals with a history of multiple concussions.

contusion   A bruise caused by a direct blow, which may cause swelling and bleeding in muscles and other body tissues.

corticosteroids   Medications that can be used to reduce or prevent swelling and irritation.

CT scan   A computed tomography scan (also called a CAT scan, for computed axial tomography); a series of X-rays taken at different levels that allows the direct three-dimensional visualization of structures inside the body.

dementia pugilistica	A brain disease similar to CTE that is primarily associated with boxers.
diffuse brain injury	Injury to cells in many areas of the brain rather than in one specific location.
dislocation	Complete disruption in the normal relationship of two bones forming a joint.
disorientation	A confused state of mind in which a person does not know where he is, who he is, or what day it is. Health professionals often speak of a normal state of mind as being oriented "times three" which refers to person, place, and time.
electro-encephalogram	A procedure that uses electrodes on the scalp to record electrical activity of the brain.
electromyography	A procedure entailing the insertion of needle electrodes into muscles to study the electrical activity of muscle and nerve fibers in order to diagnose damage to nerves or muscles.
flexion	Bending a joint toward the body.
fracture	A break in bone tissue.
hairline fracture	A thin crack in the bone.
hematoma	The collection of blood in tissues following an injury; can be life threatening when occurring in the brain.
inflammation	A localized tissue response initiated by tissue damage; symptoms include heat, redness, swelling, and pain.
laceration	A cut in the skin that is usually deep enough to require stitches.
ligament	A band of fibrous tissue that connects a bone to another bone at a joint.
magnetic resonance imaging (MRI)	A type of diagnostic radiography using electromagnetic energy to create an image of soft tissues as well as bone.
medial collateral ligament	One of the four major ligaments of the human knee. It is on the medial (inner) side of the knee joint in humans.

meniscus	C-shaped pieces of cartilage that cushion joined bones, such as the knee meniscus, which cushions the femur (thigh bone) and the tibia (shin bone).
muscle	Contractile connective tissue that provides bodily movement; a component of nearly all organs and body systems.
muscle cramp	Involuntary spasm or contraction in one or more muscles.
nonsteroidal anti-inflammatory drug (NSAID)	A class of drugs that act as pain relievers, fever reducers, and anti-inflammatories. Common NSAIDs include aspirin and ibuprofen.
orthopedics	The branch of medicine devoted to the study and treatment of the skeletal system, its joints, muscles and associated structures.
overuse injury	Any injury caused by repetitive stress that surpasses the tissue's natural repair processes.
physical therapy	The treatment of disease, injury, or deformity by physical methods such as massage, heat treatment, and exercise rather than by drugs; may be used in conjunction with medication.
plateau	A temporary or permanent leveling off in the recovery process.
prognosis	The prospect of recovery from a disease or injury as indicated by the nature and symptoms of the case.
range of motion	How far a joint can move without pain.
rehabilitation	Comprehensive program to reduce/overcome deficits following injury or illness that assists the individual to regain the optimal level of mental and physical performance.
repetitive stress injury (RSI)	An injury that happens when too much stress is repeatedly placed on a part of the body, resulting in inflammation, muscle strain, or tissue damage.
RICE	An acronym for rest, ice, compression, and elevation; a method of treatment of acute injury that is used to counteract the body's initial response to injury.
sports medicine	A field of medicine concerned with the prevention and treatment of injuries and disorders related to participation in sports.

sprain	A stretch or tear of a ligament.
strain	A stretch or tear of a muscle or tendon.
stress fracture	An overuse injury in which the body cannot repair microscopic damage to the bone as quickly as it is induced, leading to a painful, weakened bone.
tear	Where tissue is pulled or ripped apart by force.
tendinitis	Inflammation of the tendon caused by repetitive stretching.
tendon	A band of fibrous tissue that attaches muscle to bone.
tennis elbow	A condition where the outer part of the elbow becomes sore and painful, often seen in tennis players; technically called lateral epicondylitis or lateral epicondylalgia.
Tommy John surgery	The common name for a surgical procedure, technically known as ulnar collateral ligament (UCL) reconstruction, where a ligament in the medial (inside) elbow is replaced with a tendon from elsewhere in the body.
traumatic brain injury(TBI)	An injury to the brain caused by a blow to the head.
ultrasound	A diagnostic procedure using high-frequency sound waves to image organs and structures inside the body.

CHRONOLOGY

ca. 850 B.C.   A passage in Homer's *Iliad* describes a sports injury occurring during a chariot race.

ca. 500 B.C.   Greek physician Herodicus uses therapeutic exercise to help heal injuries.

ca. 100 B.C.   Galen, a Greek physician, oversees the training, diet, and medical care of Roman gladiators.

A.D. 1500s   The term *concussion* comes into use, and symptoms such as confusion, lethargy, and memory problems are described.

1780   Jean-Andre Venel builds the first orthopedic institute in Switzerland.

1845   French physician Amedee Bonnet writes treatises on tendon and muscular cuttings and joint diseases.

1851   Antonius Mathysen, a Dutch military surgeon, invents the plaster of Paris cast to help heal broken bones.

1894   Four English nurses form the Chartered Society of Physiotherapy.

1895   Englishman A.W. Mayo Robson performs the first surgical treatment of a ruptured anterior cruciate ligament (ACL).

1903	German doctor F. Lange performs the first ACL replacement using braided silk.
1917	English physician Ernest Hey-Groves performs the first ACL reconstruction using grafted thigh muscle.
1928	Dr. Harrison Stanford Martland, chief medical examiner of Essex County, New Jersey, describes tremors, slowed movement, confusion, and speech problems in boxers and introduces the term "punch drunk boxers."
1939	Helmets are made mandatory in college football.
1943	Helmets are made mandatory by the National Football League (NFL).
1966	The term *chronic traumatic encephalopathy* (CTE) appears in medical literature.
1974	Frank Jobe, an orthopedic surgeon, reconstructs pitcher Tommy John's ulnar collateral ligament and names (and trademarks) the procedure Tommy John surgery.
1979	Helmets are made mandatory for all new players in the National Hockey League. Those already in the league prior to the mandate are still allowed to play without them.
2002–2005	Pittsburgh medical examiner and forensic pathologist Bennet Omalu identifies CTE in two former professional football players.
2008	The Center for the Study of Traumatic Encephalopathy is created at Boston University School of Medicine.

2012   Professional football players file a suit against the NFL, accusing it of hiding information that linked football-related head trauma to permanent brain injuries.

2013   The family of suicide and CTE victim Junior Seau, an all-pro linebacker, file a wrongful death suit against the NFL.

ORGANIZATIONS TO CONTACT

The editors have compiled the following list of organizations concerned with the issues debated in this book. The descriptions are derived from materials provided by the organizations. All have publications or information available for interested readers. The list was compiled on the date of publication of the present volume; the information provided here may change. Be aware that many organizations take several weeks or longer to respond to inquiries, so allow as much time as possible.

American College of Sports Medicine (ACSM)
401 W. Michigan St., Indianapolis, IN 46202-3233
(317) 637-9200.
e-mail: public info@acsm.org
website: www.acsm.org

The ACSM is a sports medicine and exercise science organization dedicated to advancing and integrating scientific research to provide educational and practical applications of exercise science and sports medicine. The ACSM sponsors initiatives such as antidoping advocacy and childhood obesity prevention. The college offers several sports injury–related publications, including *Medicine & Science in Sports & Exercise, Current Sports Medicine Reports*, and *Exercise and Sport Sciences Reviews.*

American Orthopaedic Society for Sports Medicine (AOSSM)
6300 N. River Rd., Ste. 500, Rosemont, IL 60018
(847) 292-4900
fax: (847) 292-4905
e-mail: info@aossm.org
website: www.sports med.org

The American Orthopaedic Society for Sports Medicine is an international organization of orthopedic surgeons and other allied health professionals dedicated to sports medicine. The members of the AOSSM help athletes at all levels of sport to prevent and manage injury. The AOSSM's *American Journal of Sports Medicine* is a peer-reviewed scientific journal that provides a forum for independent orthopedic sports medicine research and education.

American Sports Medicine Institute (ASMI)
2660 Tenth Ave. South, Ste. 505, Birmingham, AL 35205
(205) 918-0000
e-mail: info@asmi.org
website: www.asmi.org

The ASMI is a nonprofit sports medicine research and education foundation located at St. Vincent's Hospital in Birmingham, Alabama. The mission of ASMI is to improve the understanding, prevention, and treatment of sports-related injuries through research and education. The institute's activities include providing advanced training in sports medicine to physicians and other medical specialists and conducting research in sports medicine. The ASMI website provides links to articles written by researchers funded by the institute.

Datalys Center for Sports Injury Research and Prevention
401 W. Michigan St., Ste. 500, Indianapolis, IN 46202
(317) 275-3664
website: http://datalys center.org

The mission of the Datalys Center for Sports Injury Research and Prevention is to collect and translate sports participation, injury, and treatment data into effective programs, policies, rules, and education aimed at preventing, mitigating, and treating sports injuries. The center provides organizations and policy makers with unbiased data and interpretation that can be used to make data-driven policy decisions. The organization's website offers fact sheets and publications providing relevant statistics.

International Federation of Sports Medicine (FIMS)
Maison du Sport International, Av. de Rhodanie 54, CH-1007 Lausanne, Switzerland
e-mail: headquarters -ch@fims.org
website: www.fims.org /en

FIMS is an international organization comprising national sports medicine associations from countries all over the world. The aim of FIMS is to promote the study and development of sports medicine throughout the world, preserve and improve the health of humankind through physical fitness and sports participation, and to scientifically study the natural and pathological implications of physical training and sports participation. FIMS organizes and sponsors internationally based scientific meetings, courses, congresses, and exhibits on sports medicine. The organization publishes the *International SportMed Journal* and a quarterly newsletter, the *World of Sports Medicine*.

National Alliance for Youth Sports (NAYS)
2050 Vista Pkwy.,
West Palm Beach, FL
33411
(561) 684-1141
fax: (561) 684-2546
website: www.nays.org

NAYS is a nonprofit organization that seeks to make sports safe, fun, and healthy for all children. NAYS promotes the value and importance of sports and physical activities in the emotional, physical, social, and mental development of youth and believes that participation in sports and activities develops important character traits and lifelong values. In addition, NAYS believes that the lives of youngsters can be positively impacted by participation in sports and physical activities if the adults involved have proper training and information. The organization offers a monthly electronic newsletter, a blog, and occasional webinars.

National Center for Sports Safety (NCSS)
2316 First Ave. South,
Birmingham, AL
35233
(205) 329-7535
fax: (205) 329-7526
e-mail: info@sports safety.org
website: www.sports safety.org

The NCSS promotes the importance of injury prevention and safety at all levels of youth sports through education and research. The NCSS focuses on decreasing the number and/ or severity of injuries through developing and teaching sports safety courses and collecting, analyzing, and researching injury data. The organization's website offers a full library of articles on health and nutrition, coaching and safety, and other sports-injury topics.

National Collegiate Athletic Association (NCAA)
700 W. Washington St., PO Box 6222,
Indianapolis, IN
46206-6222
(317) 917-6222
fax: (317) 917-6888
website: www.ncaa.org

The NCAA strives to protect student-athletes, focusing on both athletics and academic excellence. Part of the NCAA's mission is to provide student-athletes with a competitive environment that is safe and that ensures fair play. The NCAA establishes safety guidelines, playing rules, equipment standards, drug-testing procedures, and research into the cause of injuries to assist policy making. The organization publishes the *NCAA Champion Magazine* on a quarterly basis.

**Sports Legacy
Institute (SLI)**
PO Box 181225,
Boston, MA 02118
(781) 819-5706
fax: (781) 819-5710
e-mail: info@sports
legacy.org
website: www.sports
legacy.org

The SLI is a nonprofit organization that works to make sports safer through grassroots educational programs and is dedicated to solving the concussion crisis in sports and the military through medical research, treatment, education, and prevention. The SLI believes that the absence of awareness and education and poor concussion diagnosis and management has allowed chronic traumatic encephalopathy (CTE) to proliferate. The SLI, in partnership with Boston University School of Medicine, formed the Center for the Study of Traumatic Encephalopathy. The institute publishes a periodic newsletter.

STOP Sports Injuries
6300 N. River Rd.,
Ste. 500, Rosemont, IL
60018
(847) 655-8660
e-mail: info@stop
sportsinjuries.org
website: www.stop
sportsinjuries.org

The STOP Sports Injuries campaign was initiated by the American Orthopaedic Society for Sports Medicine partnering with the American Academy of Orthopaedic Surgeons, the American Academy of Pediatrics, the National Athletic Trainers' Association, the American Medical Society for Sports Medicine and Safe Kids USA. STOP Sports Injuries was created to help prevent athletic injuries to kids from overuse and trauma. STOP Sports Injuries provides information for parents, athletes, coaches, and health care professionals. The STOP Sports Injuries website provides public service announcements, posters, DVDs, brochures, fact sheets, and a blog.

FOR FURTHER READING

Books

Linda Carroll and David Rosner, *The Concussion Crisis: Anatomy of a Silent Epidemic.* New York: Simon & Schuster, 2012.

Will Carroll, *Saving the Pitcher.* Lanham, MD: Ivan R. Dee, 2007.

Gay Culverhouse, *Throwaway Players: Concussion Crisis from Pee Wee Football to the NFL.* North Fayette, PA: Behler, 2011.

Tom Farrey, *Game On.* Bristol, CT: ESPN, 2008.

Mark Hyman, *Until It Hurts: America's Obsession with Youth Sports and How It Harms Our Kids.* Boston: Beacon, 2010.

Mary Ann Keatley and Laura L. Whittemore, *Understanding Mild Traumatic Brain Injury (MTBI): An Insightful Guide to Symptoms, Treatments, and Redefining Recovery.* Boulder, CO: Brain Injury Hope Foundation, 2010.

Donald Kirkendall, *Soccer Anatomy.* Champaign, IL: Human Kinetics, 2011.

Robert Marx, *The ACL Solution.* New York: Demos Medical, 2012.

Frederick O. Muller and Robert C. Cantu, *Football Fatalities and Catastrophic Injuries, 1931–2008.* Durham, NC: Carolina Academic, 2010.

Michael Sokolove, *Warrior Girls: Protecting Our Daughters Against the Injury Epidemic in Women's Sports.* New York: Simon & Schuster, 2008.

Benjamin Nathaniel Ungar, *Too Successful? Tommy John Surgery and Perceptions of Success in Sports Medicine.* Honors Thesis. Cambridge, MA: Harvard University, 2009

Brad Walker, *The Anatomy of Sports Injuries.* Berkeley, CA: North Atlantic, 2007.

Periodicals and Internet Sources

Mitch Albom, "NFL Players Pay a Price After the Cheering Stops," *Detroit Free Press,* June 10, 2012.

Jim Barlow, "After Concussion, Teen Athletes Recover Slowly," Futurity.org, January 7, 2013. www.futurity.org/health-medicine /after-concussion-teen-athletes-recover-slowly.

Laura Beil, "Smack Upside the Head," *Men's Health,* March 2012.

Maureen Cavanaugh, Hank Crook, and Kathy Boccela, "In Chesco, a Cluster of Concussions: Girls Suffering Them at a High Rate in Soccer," Philly.com, May 14, 2012. http://articles .philly.com/2012-05-14/news/31690091_1_girls-soccer-concus sions-head-injuries.

Katherine Chretien, "Why I Won't Risk My Child's Brain for Football," *USA Today,* April 28, 2011.

Maggie Clark, "States Find Laws Against Sports Head Injuries Tricky to Enact," Stateline (news service of the Pew Charitable Trusts), July 19, 2012. www.pewstates.org/projects/stateline /headlines/states-find-laws-against-sports-head-injuries-tricky -to-enact-85899405995.

Steven DeKosky, Milos Ikonomovic, and Sam Gandy, "Traumatic Brain Injury—Football, Warfare, and Long-Term Effects," *New England Journal of Medicine,* September 30, 2010.

Mark Edmundson, "Do Sports Build Character or Damage It?," *Chronicle of Higher Education,* January 15, 2012.

Carrie Gann, "Down a Kidney? Don't Rule Out Sports," *Medical Unit* (blog), ABC News, June 18, 2012. http://abcnews.go .com/blogs/health/2012/06/18/down-a-kidney-dont-rule-out -sports.

Jamie Gumbrecht, "Dealing with the Aftermath of a Serious High School Sports Injury," CNN.com, October 4, 2011. www .cnn.com/201l/US/10/04/cnnheroes.sports.injuries/index.html ?hpt=hp_c1.

Gina Kolata, "Treat Me, but No Tricks Please," *New York Times,* January 6, 2010.

Jere Longman, "For Women in Sports, A.C.L. Injuries Take Toll," *New York Times,* March 26, 2011.

Susie Madrak, "If Concussions Can Devastate NFL Players, Why Are We Letting Children with Multiple Concussions Keep Playing Sports?," CrooksandLiars.com, May 15, 2012. http://crooksandliars.com/susie-madrak/if-concussions-can-devastate-nfl-play.

Mark Maske, "Concussions in NFL Down from Last Season Because of Kickoff Rule Change, Study Finds," *Washington Post*, August 7, 2012.

Terence Moore, "The Dissenter: Pro Football's Loneliest Position," CNN.com, June 1, 2012. www.cnn.com/2012/06/01/us/lester-hayes-nfl/index.html.

Abby Ohlheiser, "NFL Player Junior Seau Had Degenerative Brain Disease CTE at Time of Death," *Slate*, January 10, 2013. www.slate.com/blogs/the_slatest/2013/01/10/junior_seau_suicide_nfl_player_had_brain_disease_cte_at_time_of_death_according.html?wpisrc=newsletter_jcr:content.

Vikki Ortiz Healy and Erin Meyer, "Boy's Baseball Death Spotlights Need for Tracking Youth Sports Injuries," *Chicago Tribune*, April 20, 2012.

Peter Richmond, "Quadriplegic Chic Kelly Just Wants Enough Money to Pay for His Care," *Sports Illustrated*, July 28, 2011. http://sportsillustrated.cnn.com/2011/writers/the_bonus/07/27/chic.kelly/index.html#ixzz2Ijwn7OMM.

Jake Simpson, "Why the Nationals Are Right to Shut Down Stephen Strasburg," *Atlantic*, August 22, 2012.

Jon Styf, "Can Football Be Fatal?," *Beaumont (TX) Enterprise*, April 11, 2011. www.beaumontenterprise.com/sports/article/Can-football-be-fatal-1331886.php#page-2.

David Zinczenko, "It Only Looks Dangerous," *New York Times*, April 1, 2011.

INDEX

A

AAP (American Academy of Pediatrics), 75
ACEP (American College of Emergency Physicians), 80
ACL tears. *See* Anterior cruciate ligament tears
Adolescents. *See* Children/adolescents
Aikman, Troy, 96
Akizuki, Ken, 44, 45, 47, 48
American Academy of Pediatrics (AAP), 69, 75
American College of Emergency Physicians (ACEP), 80
American Horse Slaughter Prevention Act (proposed), 12–13
American Journal of Sports Medicine, 49
American Orthopedic Society for Sports Medicine, 80
Andrews, James R., 71
Anterior cruciate ligament (ACL) tears, 24–29, *26,* 81–82
Arcaro, Eddie, 9
Archives of Disease in Childhood (journal), 71
Asthma, exercise-induced, 82–83
Athletic equipment safety standards, 107

B

Bakhos, Lisa, 76
Barbaro (race horse), 9–10
Benson, Kris, 45
Berg, Lindsey, 60–61, *65*
Bernick, Charles, 109
Bettman, Gary, 37

Boogaard, Derek, 37
Boston University, 38
Boxers, brain injuries in, 109–116
Brady, Tom, 28
Brain injuries, 18–20
   in boxers/mixed martial arts fighters, 109–116
   youth emergency room visits for, 37, *77*
   See also Chronic traumatic encephalopathy; Concussion
Branch, David, 37
Brenner, Joel S., 69–71
British Journal of Sport Medicine, 85
Brody, Jane E., 68
Bryant, Kobe, 61
Bursitis, 18
Bynum, Andrew, 61

C

Canadian Medical Association Journal, 36–37
Cantu, Robert, 33, 34, 39, 40–41
Carroll, Will, 42
Casson, Ira, 91, 93
CDC (Centers for Disease Control and Prevention), 37, 38, 81, 105
Center for Injury Research and Policy, 112
Centers for Disease Control and Prevention (CDC), 37, 38, 81, 105
Children/adolescents
   annual emergency room visits due to traumatic brain injuries in, 37, *77*
   numbers playing sports/injured annually, *73*